COLLECTIVE DREAMS

COLLECTIVE DREAMS
POLITICAL IMAGINATION & COMMUNITY

Keally D. McBride

The Pennsylvania State University Press
University Park, Pennsylvania

Library of Congress Cataloging-in-Publication Data

McBride, Keally D.
Collective dreams : political imagination and community / Keally D. McBride.
    p.   cm.
Includes bibliographical references and index.
ISBN 0-271-02688-X (alk. paper)
1. Community.
2. Community—Political aspects.
3. Community life—United States—Case studies.
I. Title.

HM756.M33 2005
307´.01—dc22
2004028122

Copyright © 2005 The Pennsylvania State University
All rights reserved
Printed in the United States of America
Published by The Pennsylvania State University Press,
University Park, PA 16802-1003

The Pennsylvania State University Press
is a member of the
Association of American University Presses.

It is the policy of
The Pennsylvania State University Press
to use acid-free paper. This book is printed on
Natures Natural, containing 50% post-consumer waste
and meets the minimum requirements of American
National Standard for Information Sciences—
Permanence of Paper for Printed Library Material,
ANSI Z39.48–1992.

Dedicated to the Life and Imagination of
MIKE ROGIN

CONTENTS

ACKNOWLEDGMENTS ix

INTRODUCTION 1

1 The Politics of Imagining Communities 9

2 A Room Full of Mirrors: Community and the Promise of Identity 23

3 Habits of the Hearth: Families and Politics in Theory and Practice 43

4 Citizens Without States? Bringing Community into Institutions 59

5 Consuming Community 85

6 Utopian Vision as Commodity Fetish: Social Imagineering in Postmodern Capitalism 111

7 Community in Practice 121

WORKS CITED 141

INDEX 151

ACKNOWLEDGMENTS

There were multitudes who provided advice and encouragement at key points in the genesis of this book. First and foremost, John Zarobell read and talked about every draft. He would get up so I could sleep and he never stopped thinking the project mattered. My advisors at University of California, Berkeley, Hanna Pitkin, Mary Ryan, and Paul Thomas, all provided terrific guidance, and Mike Rogin was a model mentor. Nancy Hirshmann and Mary Katzenstein gave much needed advice at Cornell University. Readers Peggy Kohn and William Caspary and editor Sandy Thatcher gave judicious criticism for the Pennsylvania State University Press. Many thanks to friends and colleagues who have read and talked about the project: Kevin Bundy, Jesse Goldhammer, Alexa Sand, Deborah Zafman, the "Gender Gang" at Berkeley, Nils Gilman, Sarah Kennel, Gaston Alonso, and Martyn Thompson. My students have also been a source of ideas and fresh thinking; my thanks in particular to the "Citizenship in a Changing World" seminar at Temple University and the "Feminist Research Methods" class at Tulane University. Betsy asked the usual piercing questions and Linza always seemed to show up at just the right time to take over with the kids.

INTRODUCTION

This is a book about imagining a better world. While I was growing up, I moved every year. I was a spectator of the world around me, but everyone else looked as though he or she were a participant. I assumed that if only I was one of them, I would feel at home, I would belong. Like me, many people lament the fact that they have never felt part of a "real community." Some people forget about this longing, others spend a lot of energy trying to figure out how, or where, they might feel at home in the world. This rootlessness is all too often blamed upon the technological mobility of modernism. But in looking at the tradition of political theory, we find that fostering communal life was a primary goal even in the earliest works of the tradition. Community life has always figured prominently in ideal political orders.

Delineating how we imagine community today is an urgent project. Ideals of community express a virtually universal longing for humane sociality on the most basic level. The desire for belonging is the impetus behind a great deal of political imagination. Somehow, though, these critiques—these acts of political imagination—become neutralized. My goal is to look at community as both a predominant form of political imagination today and a response to liberal individualism and capitalism. On one level, community is assumed to be an alternative to these social orders. But it is facile to think that imagination can exist untouched by the circumstances that produce it. A purely oppositional imagination is impossible. Imagination is frequently about desire, specifically desire for something that is not immediately evident. I want to explore the tension between political reality and political possibility revealed by the way we imagine community. Following in the tradition of Walter Benjamin, *Collective Dreams* studies the effects of culture on consciousness and the political quandaries that ensue.

Imagination itself, as opposed to its products, is generally not studied in political science. But it is our best tool for changing the world. Imagining is shaped by material and social circumstances. This is not to argue that imagination is somehow tainted or co-opted by society, as is suggested in the work of Herbert Marcuse (1964). My outlook is ultimately a more optimistic one than this. Imagination is best served when there is a productive interplay between possibility and actuality. To say that imagination is affected socially is to emphasize one of the preconditions of its power. However, sometimes imagination does become neutralized or captured by social circumstances. Therefore, I include a study of how consumer capitalism shapes, and can frustrate, imagination.

Ideals of community provide my case study of political imagination because many people commonly point to community as an aspect of their life that is either missing or undernourished. Community is also important politically in the United States as it has guided recent attempts to reform both social and political institutions: community sentencing, community policing, and faith-based initiatives are just a few prominent examples. Ideals of community also serve as guides for how we build new environments and evaluate and repair old ones. Urban planners and suburban developers are preoccupied with planned communities, community development, and community restoration. Community seems to be an ascendant concept at this historic juncture. I offer different explanations throughout the book as to how ideals of community respond to identity politics, capitalism, and liberalism.

As an ideal, community seems to be defined more as what we do *not* have rather than carrying any concrete attributes reflecting what we are a part of. Community is a word that is used frequently, and therefore apparently requires no definition or explanation. Just as (practically) no one demands elaboration when we refer to this country as democratic,[1] very few would think to list the criteria that make it possible to refer to a place or group of people as a "community." Yet asking what makes communities, and why they are currently considered important, can reveal much about how we view public life and politics in this country.

Looking at community in order to understand public life seems counterintuitive because community is frequently understood as an intimate, private sphere, as opposed to the public pursuit of politics. Community sounds like a welcome respite from the mechanisms of state, market, and

---

1. See Stephen Eric Bronner's *Idea's in Action: Political Tradition in the Twentieth Century* for an excellent discussion of the misuses of the word "democratic." In many ways his suggestion that "Democracy has become the answer to every question and the solution to every problem" (Bronner 1999, 18) echoes my own argument about the concept of community in contemporary political discourse.

bureaucracy. The understanding of community as the alternative to the impersonal modern world originated with Ferdinand Tönnies's classic work, *Gemeinschaft und Gesellschaft* (1957). In this sense, then, the appearance of community in political rhetoric is a marker of disenchantment with politics and the public realm.

This oppositionality makes the concept of community attractive to those of all political persuasions. For example, the practice of community sentencing sounds good to those who see it as a way to get tough on crime and to those who want a more personalized form of justice alike. Justice can be meted out in the name of an injured community, or justice can be mandated in the interest of healing an injured community—of which the offender is a part. Community is imagined as specific, embedded, and particular, in opposition to the universalizing institutions of market and state.

Another characteristic that makes community a unique concept is that it implies intimate transcendence of self. Communities are both personal and interpersonal: they enable ways of being involved with others without losing what makes oneself distinct. In contrast, society or universalism emphasizes belonging at the expense of identity or particularity. Community becomes the ideal mediation between self and society, a socially embedded, yet particularized, location. However, this understanding of community rests upon Tönnies's (1957) opposition of society and community. I contest this opposition of community with society, and suggest instead that how we attempt to delineate community and society reveals our understanding and experience of both.

After years of studying ideas and plans for communities, it is striking to see how varied they are and how central a role they play in many visions of politics. It is tempting to try to present a catalog of all the different ideas of community that are currently circulating. Gerard Delanty (2003) has recently done so, in an extremely comprehensive book, so here I will offer only a brief typological analysis to provide the background for the discussion that will follow.

Civic Community. Political theorists following in the tradition of Tocqueville argue that institutions of political liberalism need to be complemented with vigorous community activism in order to maintain democracy. Without concerted public participation, the institutions of representative democracy pursue their own interests. In order to maintain the democratic elements in liberalism and fight the centralization of power, the public needs to be informed, active, and easily mobilized to protect its interests. Benjamin Barber (1984, 1988, 1998) and Michael Sandel (1982, 1996a, 1996b) are two prominent advocates of this position, where community is seen as a crucial element in revitalizing political freedom and democratic government through public participation. Drawing on ancient political theory, they also argue that public life is inherently rewarding and that human existence is impoverished without the opportunity to shape one's environment.

Communities of Resistance. This is the version of grassroots activism that follows in the tradition of Marxist collectivity. Organized local communities provide resistance to corporatism and globalism. While global capitalism and international organizations strip individuals and local communities of their particular traditions and identities, collectives band together to assert their rights and to maintain their different values in opposition to globalization. The language of community pervades contemporary activism—on both the right and left. The right, also hostile to government administration, though for different reasons, asserts community control as the alternative to government. Oftentimes this juxtaposition is adopted in academic work, as in Seyla Benhabib's book *The Claims of Culture*, which positions local, particular communities in opposition to universal, global capitalism. She offers a vision of an ethical and equal globalization if we break down the antinomy and instead see ourselves as a gigantic "community of interdependence" (Benhabib 2002, 35–37). For Benhabib, enlarging the commitments and particularism implied by community to a global scope provides the corrective to universalism.

Communities of Difference. One outgrowth of identity politics is to recognize the importance of community for supporting a marginalized identity. Communities are emphasized to make visible and express the collective strength of a previously "unseen" population. In this school of thought, community is viewed as providing a political and expressive function, as in the works of Audre Lorde (1984) and Bernice Johnson Reagon (1983). The link between identity and politics is reflected in these ideas about community: communities are crafted together through action instead of "naturally" occurring. This view of community is now common in activist circles and everyday political activity, as well as academic work.

Naturalized Community. In contrast to the group above, theorists of this framework point to our natural inclination to form communities and suggest that communities exist before political action. It is the responsibility of politics to recognize and support already existing communities. To distinguish themselves from a variant of tribalism, these theorists emphasize that communities can be inclusive and heterogeneous. Mary Ann Glendon (1987, 1991, 1997), Philip Selznick (1992, 1995), and Amitai Etzioni (1990, 1993,

1996a, 1996b) propose that institutional shifts can help communities to flourish. They argue that increased social stability and personal fulfillment in the United States will result from more community-friendly policies and laws.

Communities of Particularism. Some feminist and critical race theorists have seized upon community as the corrective to liberal individualism. In contrast to the universal or neutral subject of political liberalism, communities recognize the particular characteristics and needs of their members. Arguing that universalism occludes the specific needs of different groups and maintains a scrim of neutrality that serves discrimination, theorists such as Anne Phillips (1993), Jane Flax (1987, 1993), and Iris Marion Young (1990, 1994, 1997) have looked at using community as an alternative medium for achieving political justice and citizenship. Communities are offered as substitutes for the impersonal institutions of democratic liberalism that have failed to create equality through universalism.

Hybrid Communities. This vision of community emphasizes the heterogeneity of both communities and the selves that are constructed within them. Combining the insights of naturalized and postmodern community ideals, this view posits a correspondence between hybrid communities and multiplicitous selves. Trinh T. Mihn-Ha (1989, 1991), Maria Lugones (1994), and Gloria Anzaldúa (1987) all articulate an alternative vision of communities that recognize our necessarily fragmented, evolving personal identities—situated on borderlands and constructed through difference. An emphasis upon difference and heterogeneity points to the politics of exclusion and oppositional identity construction that predominate political life. The goal is to have politics recognize both self and community as incomplete and evolving, allowing a true politics of difference to flourish.

Postmodern Communities. Largely in reaction to the idea of naturalized communities, William Connolly (1991), Jean-Luc Nancy (1991), Giorgio Agamben (1993), and William Corlett (1989) have argued for a view of communities as inherently agonistic and unsettled. Humans do create communities, but these communities fail and, indeed, should fail. "Complete" communities are attempts to shelter ourselves from difference, create a safe haven from politics, and provide for a confirmation of self. Similar to theorists of hybrid communities, this group emphasizes the socially constructed and always evolving nature of identity. But these theorists emphasize discord and disharmony in their vision of community more than its fragmentation. Here communities echo the struggle of politics and, in this sense, differ from the other theories of community I have outlined. Bonnie Honig (1993, 2001), Elizabeth Frazer (1999), and Frazer and Nicola Lacey (1993) make related arguments, arguing for an agonistic view of politics as opposed to a consensual one. These thinkers combine the presence of community with a combative view of politics, whereas frequently other thinkers offer community as the alternative to agonistic politics.

Why study how we imagine communities? Why not examine how we build them? Or why we don't? I think the answer to these last two questions lies in the answer to the first one. What if the way we imagine communities prevents us from building them, or even serves as an alternative for doing so? Imagination does not always inspire or guarantee direct correspondence in reality. This does not mean it has somehow failed or is unimportant, however. Imagination can compensate for reality—here it is called fantasy. Or imagination can constitute reality, for example when an invented threat can create real defenses. Additionally, imagination can critique reality, as when we imagine that there are other ways to live our lives. Although I've just separated all three of these possibilities, in practice it is much more difficult to do so and these functions are not mutually exclusive.

This is why I am more interested in the effects of how we imagine community than in how we define it. As my mapping of ideas of community above suggests, there is strong disagreement about how community should properly be understood: universal or particular, exclusive or inclusive, traditional or progressive, constructed or essentialist? Rather than champion one definition over another, I suggest we focus on the fact that so many people utilize conceptions of community in their version of politics, whether it be traditional, progressive, radical, patriarchal, or feminist. The battle over whose definition of community is right will never end. But we can start to explain how and why community plays such a crucial function in American political discourse on right, left, margin, and center.

Surveying this list of possible conceptions of community, there are clear advantages and disadvantages in each way of imagining it. I do not favor one vision at the expense of all the rest, nor is it my intention to argue which version of community is "correct," most practical, useful, liberatory, or appropriate. Rather, I am interested in how all of these visions try to remake the world through imagining alternatives. I bring three goals to conducting this study of ideals of community. The first is to articulate what these alternative ideals say about our current system. The second is to see how imagining change is influenced by the very conditions that produce the desire for change. The last is to examine why concepts of community have not been more effective in creating social change.

This study is also concerned with the importance and potential of imagination in politics generally. Imagination is a crucial yet underexplored aspect of politics that is situated in a particularly dynamic location. The first chapter of the book explicates this position more thoroughly, but here is a sketch of how I place imagination. On one continuum, imagination is situated between individual and society, meaning that it is something that is both socially influenced and experienced and articulated in different ways by different people. On a second continuum, imagination is placed between ideal and materiality. Imagination both resists and is influenced by the world as it currently exists. It sits at the point of intersection between individual freedom and social membership, possibility and actuality. This convergence makes imagination a potent political tool for both critique and change. Hence a conception of imagination as a tool, as well as a concern for community as an ideal, drives this discussion.

The first two chapters look at the political function of imagination and what happens when imagination becomes unmoored from the world. This is a particularly interesting question in the context of ideals of community. After all, if we live in a world without communities, how is it that we are able to imagine them? Chapters 3 and 4 examine how ideals of community have been particularly attractive in attempting to reform the political institutions of liberalism. I argue that the characteristics of community as they are idealized make them rather unsuitable for achieving institutional reform, and suggest alternative ways that communities can change liberal institutions. Chapters 5 and 6 ask how the world influences imagination as well as how it may neutralize it. Here I am particularly interested in the fate of political imagination in an era of consumer capitalism. Commodity fetishism provides a unique obstacle for the realization of imagination that should be carefully considered. Finally, I conclude with an empirical study of a community to serve as a counterweight to the study of Celebration, Florida, the Disney-built community discussed in Chapter 5. A brief study of the elements of community at work in West Philadelphia serves to tie together theory and practice, imagination and materiality in my consideration of community.

William Connolly mused, "Perhaps a fruitful task for the political intellectual is to interrogate unconscious dimensions of the political imagination through which contemporary possibilities and impossibilities are delineated" (Connolly 1995, xxx). Looking into the ways we imagine community can demonstrate how we understand what is possible. Releasing the bonds upon imagination can help to create new dreams, and new worlds.

1

THE POLITICS OF
IMAGINING COMMUNITIES

The term "community" has a paradoxical presence in our everyday discourse. While many people lament not being part of a "real community," they nonetheless use the word repeatedly to refer to groups. The problem became clearer to me after reading Hervé Varenne's study of Appleton, Wisconsin, titled *Americans Together* (1977). This French scholar began his sociological analysis by regretfully reporting that he was not able to find a "real community" in Appleton—but then went on to describe the sociological groups that he studied as "communities" anyway. Clearly the word "community" carries both normative and descriptive weight. Curiously, the ideals that are associated with the concept of community do not seem to be found in the groups that we call communities. How is it that we can nod our heads about the lack of community feeling in the United States, yet every day hear references to "the African American community," "the financial community," or "the gay and lesbian community"?

One could argue that we toss the word around to designate groups that are clearly not unified or singular only because we have lost any sense of what a "real community" is. But it is more persuasive to recognize that there is a tension between the normative understanding of communities and the everyday experience of them. The normative understanding of the word is that communities are based on shared experience, identity, or location, and that membership is fulfilling in the sense that one's own identity is reflected back in a positive way. Those who are within communities find support and acceptance from their membership. It is this normative dimension of the word that signals respect for an otherwise disenfranchised group when we call it a community. The trace elements of our idealized community follow the word in its "descriptive" task. It is the ideal that makes the descriptive use of "community" omnipresent.

All of us belong to groups that could be called communities in the sense that these groups are based upon shared beliefs or experiences. Yet communal experience is very rarely without obstacles, struggle, or disappointment. Those who belong to "the African American community" or "the feminist community" know exactly how divided, contentious, and necessarily partial membership in these groups is. So the ideal of community does not originate from or necessarily correspond to a collective experience.

The two most common ways of interpreting this distinction between the experience and the ideal of communities is that the ideal is either utopian or nostalgic. "Community" as an ideal is an more updated version of Thomas More's sixteenth-century *Utopia* (2001). Utopian longings are, by their nature, unachievable. To long for community is just another way of longing for what we can't have—chasing after a lack. This particular interpretation is fueled by the dynamic I have mentioned in the introduction: we more readily designate groups of which we are *not* a part "communities." The ideal recedes in inverse proportion to our experience of the real. For instance, someone who is not directly involved may perceive that there is a strong sense of community among those participating in theatrical performance in a particular town. But the persons who are involved know that there are multiple groups who differ according to venue, philosophy, type of production, and so forth. There is not one community, but rather many. Communities function as utopias located on a horizon, receding as we draw near them.

Some have argued that the true function of a utopia is to keep us from becoming complacent with the present. It is its very inachievability that makes it serve as effective political critique. This observation has also been made about the ideal of community. For example, Jean-Luc Nancy embraces "the inoperable community," saying that communities should simultaneously pursue and reject the idea of community (Nancy 1991). The pursuit of commonalty leads us to a form of "being-in-common," which I understand as interpersonal engagement. We relate to one another toward the goal of joining together. But if this connection is achieved in its most extreme form, communities evolve into a "common being." This is when organic unity is achieved and community is no longer a matter of joining disparate entities together, but rather is the merger of many into one. Singularity precludes the possibility of interconnected plurality. A community of one is impossible. Hence the achievement of community is possible only in the gap between idealized and real communities. Nancy's description differs from the traditional understanding of utopia in his assumption that it is possible to achieve an "operable community." Nonetheless, we can take Nancy's work and recognize that a similar dynamic is in play: community provides an ideal, and whether that ideal is achievable or not, it is the fact that the ideal directs our actions toward itself that matters more than its actual realization.

Another way to understand community is as a purely nostalgic concept. Nostalgia is another form of imagining, but one that is grounded in an imaginary past rather than an imaginary future. This formulation of community can be traced to Ferdinand Tönnies (1957), who argued that community, based upon concrete and organic relationships, preceded the more abstract forms of associationalism that he calls society. Tönnies is frequently invoked as a sort of critical modernization theorist who describes what seems to be an inevitable shift from one form of satisfying sociality to another form that is less so.

Yet this understanding of community has problems. First, not all people share a vision of community as something to be recovered from the past. Many theorists of community, and I have selected many feminists as contemporary representatives of this category, look to the future as the only place to actualize ideals of community. Idealized communities of the past often disastrously excluded those who were perceived as different, or strictly regulated the lives of those within them, particularly the choices available to women. Very few feminists would invoke the ideal of community in a nostalgic sense.

The second problem with purely nostalgic ideals of community is that this conception obscures the characteristics that mark these dreams of community as our own. Dreams of an alternative world are always critiques of the present one. Ideals of community are located in the here and now, though they seek to either rescue the past or define the future. These ideals of community are products of the present, as well as attempts to change it. By creating these ideals, we both reflect and shape our world. For example, as I will discuss in Chapters 3 and 4, many feminist thinkers are aware of the problems with idealizing the family, but are less cautious when it comes to foreseeing the problems of "civil society." Similarly, French feminists see possibilities in the state due to their political traditions, while American feminists see very few.

What these two interpretations suggest is that looking at the ideal of community can not only tell us about our own time, what we think is missing, and how we try to develop answers, but also more generally about the function of imagination in politics. Community as an ideal, either nostalgic or utopian, has not been achieved, nor will it ever be. This does not mean that as an ideal it will not inspire dissatisfaction, critique, and, one hopes, change. But this imagining, while not absolutely constrained by historical reality, nonetheless reflects it. Dreams of community are generated by our contemporary experiences and inevitably reflect them. One can also transcend these experiences through the vehicle of imagination, and thereby stage an intervention in contemporary life.

It would be understandable to look at this tension between the normative and descriptive implications of community and dismiss the ideal as hopelessly utopian and out of touch with material or collective reality. Yet is it is precisely the imaginary quality of community that is politically significant. Sheldon Wolin observed that vision or imagination plays a central role in the practice of political theory. Through fancy, construction, and imagination, theorists were able to illuminate the basis of political order (Wolin 1960, 18). Neither Rousseau nor Locke ever lived in the state of nature, nor did More actually visit a place called Utopia. One goal of political theory is to present the world as it is, and sometimes doing so means manipulating the way that we see it through stories or imagination. On the other hand, Wolin comments that imagination has also "been the means by which the political theorist has sought to transcend history" (19). Ideals of community embody this dynamic as well. The ideal of community allows us to leap out of our given lives and imagine something different. This is not to say that the two functions of imagined communities are unrelated or somehow pitted one against the other. The oppositional potential is not lost through its reflective tendency. On the contrary, it is the fact that imagination engages both the ideal and the real that gives it such transformative potential. Political imagination serves as an intermediary between ideal and real, or theory and practice, connected to both but encapsulated by neither. At least, this is what the political imagination *ideally* accomplishes.

Finally, political theorists can rapidly assemble a list of the alternative ways of constructing and organizing a society according to different models of administration and economics. But the ideal of community is something that is palpable to many people; it is a critique that many can and have employed as a response to contemporary life. Constructing ideals of community is one kind of political imagining that a significant portion of the population engages in and therefore it deserves extended consideration.

IMAGINATION AND COMMUNITY IN MODERN LIFE

Let me explore a bit further the relationship between imagination, community, and politics. Tönnies developed his still-influential typology of community/society by asserting that communities were "real" associations as opposed to the more "abstract" forms of sociality in mass society. "The relationship itself, and also the resulting association, is conceived of either as real and organic life—this is the essential characteristic of the Gemeinschaft (community); or as imaginary and mechanical structure—this is the concept of Gesellschaft" (Tönnies 1957, 33). Tönnies has been frequently interpreted as saying that society replaces immediate relationships (community) with more abstract and impersonal ones. Through nation-building, the growth of mass journalism, and industrialization, society comes to replace community. Rather than association being based on face-to-face relations, society is "mere coexistence of people independent of each other" (34).

However, if we revisit this passage, we can arrive at a different understanding with the emphasis that community "*is conceived* as real and organic." Hence, rather than a historical movement from association based upon real or concrete association to a larger society based upon abstract or imagined coexistence, we have different forms of belonging that are based upon differently imagined grounds.

Benedict Anderson captures this movement quite brilliantly in his book on nationalism, *Imagined Communities* (Anderson 1983). The argument is well-known enough not to detail here, but certain aspects of it will elucidate my point. In looking at prenational cultures, Anderson observes that dynastic realms and religious communities were based upon literal understandings of their uniting features. Mass was said in Latin because it was considered to be the actual word of God. Kings' bodies provided the corporeal representation of their sovereignty, and expanding territory was accomplished through intermarriage and miscegenation: the biological merger of two royals was needed to legitimate empiric ambitions. Yet cultural shifts in the understanding of time and the development of print journalism allowed for people to imagine themselves as connected to others through what Anderson calls "simultaneity" and the market of mass media such as newspapers. The nation, Anderson reminds us, is imaginary. But it proclaims itself rooted in empirical and impersonal social relations. "At the same time, the newspaper reader, observing exact replicas of his own paper being consumed by his subway, barbershop, or residential neighbors, is continually reassured that the imagined world is visibly rooted in everyday life" (36). It is not that prenational communities were real and national ones unreal. Both eras of belonging were developed along fictive bases, supported by the cultural beliefs and practices of the time. The nation may be an imaginary community, but this does not mean that our experience of nationalism is somehow unreal.

What is particularly compelling is how Anderson roots different forms of imagination in material culture. Different worlds create different forms and ways of imagining. He is able to overcome the dichotomy between ideal and real by pointing out the material basis of cultural imagination. Imagination can be served or bolstered by the world. Anderson points out that newspapers provide the concrete referent for a sense of simultaneity in nations—they make the imagined community seem grounded empirically. Similarly, he also transcends this division by pointing out that the implications of imagination are not entirely psychological or somehow confined to our imaginations. People will die for a nation, regardless of whether it is an imaginary form of belonging. Imaginary memberships lead people to make concrete decisions and act in particular ways. The imaginary does affect practice, even if it is not perfectly embodied within it.

Looking at the history of political thought, we see clearly that imagining communities plays a central role in the vocation of political theory. This is important to remember, lest we think we have only begun to imagine sociality as a compensation for losing sociality in practice. Tönnies and Anderson suggest that in the modern era, imagined communities take on a different cast. They become more impersonal, or, to provide a more positive connotation, more universal and less specified. We have imagined communities for centuries, but the contents of these visions have changed over time to reflect their eras. For example, Tönnies and Anderson point out that one characteristic of modernity is the movement toward having communities based upon abstract relations rather than organic ones. How do our imagined communities relate to our particular era in late modernity?

Some thinkers have argued that our conception of community today is too weak, and this is why we feel alienated. Liberalism imagines us as independent entities, and hence we have become such. Proponents of this view want to resuscitate older ways of conceiving communities as a way of recapturing a different era of social organization. This line of inquiry suggests that we need to return to a more organic community—emphasizing that if the imagined basis of the community is "more concrete," the community itself will become stronger. But there are two problems with this impulse. First, it falls into the pattern of seeing community as real and society as fictive, when each era is instead based on a different imagining. It therefore ignores the fictive bases of organic unity, in effect, presenting the story of community as truth. Second, this position underestimates the efficacy of the current dominant imagined sociality: society. As abstract and impersonal and thin as this form of imagined community seems under scrutiny, it still generates human actions every day. For instance, we pay taxes to a government that is virtually faceless, send money to charities for disaster victims in countries we have never seen, and recycle in the interest of future generations. Liberalism does provide a social organization, admittedly one based upon individualism. It is the genius of modern forms of social cohesion that they are not seen as membership or as requiring sacrifice. To overlook this fact would be to underestimate the task at hand in creating an alternative order based upon communities.

It is equally important to emphasize that Anderson's and Tönnies's work demonstrates that imagined communities are not necessarily in opposition to societies and politics based upon individualism. Quite the contrary, imagined communities have been an integral element in liberal individualism from the very start. Therefore, not any or every imagined community will necessarily contest the individualist world view. This means we must take care to examine how imagined communities function, what form of politics they suggest, and how they relate to the material order of the era. Only by looking at how imagined communities interact with a contemporary world order can we determine whether they serve to bolster the current order or to challenge it. It is my belief that frequently, the ways we imagine community serve to reinforce the contemporary order, almost in a dialectical fashion. Certain forms of imagined communities as described by Tönnies and Anderson serve as the social framework that makes having a society based upon individualism function. This dynamic is similar to the one identified by Michael Walzer in an article on liberalism and communitarianism (Walzer 1990)—the two philosophies exist in a sort of symbiotic tension with one another, providing a corrective when necessary. Liberalism needs communitarianism to survive, even thrive.

Political theorists have been involved in imagining communities for centuries. This is not an activity unique to our era, nor should it be understood as a particular lack of community today that leads us to dream up communities. While the activity of envisioning communities has crossed eras, each imagined community both reflects and attempts to shape its particular historical moment. We need to look at imagined communities today as a product of, reflection of, and potential intervention in liberal individualist politics. But not all imagined communities necessarily do so: some visions of community have been integral to maintaining our individualistic society. However, it is this location between ideal and material that makes political imagination such a potentially powerful tool in shaping experience. It is my task to look at how we imagine communities and how these visions, which reflect our era, can become thwarted in their oppositionality, then to suggest ways that we can overcome these problems. For the remainder of this chapter, I will elaborate upon the unique political function served by imagination when it maintains a dynamic relationship to both idealism and material conditions; or, in more common parlance, when it negotiates between theory and practice.

INDIVIDUAL VERSUS SOCIAL IMAGINATION

Imagination is frequently viewed as an entirely individual activity. George Kateb has explored the centrality of imagination in politics, publishing an article hypothesizing that the disasters of the twentieth century, such as genocide and the two World Wars, were due to imagination. To be more exact, he describes two different kinds of imagination that together created the dismal history of the twentieth century. Kateb begins by noting that "human beings have always been creatures who live in their imagination and who also refuse, when it suits them, to exercise their imagination. We have the inborn mental capacity to make the absent present (on one hand) and (on the other) the present absent" (Kateb 2002, 486). He labels the first propensity, to make the absent present, the hyperactive or aggressive imagination. People who tend toward this variety are individuals who have a particular vision, and who use this vision to guide them in remaking the world. Hitler and Stalin spring to mind immediately as individuals with such imaginations, though it could be argued that even slightly more benign figures like Ronald Reagan also expended energy in shaping the world to match a personal vision. Although Kateb laments the silence of the canon of political theory in addressing the imagination, Engels's "Socialism: Utopian and Scientific" also contains a vivid description of this form of imagination when describing the leaders of the French Revolution: "It was a time when, as Hegel says, the world stood upon its head; first in the sense that the human head, and the principles arrived at by its thoughts, claimed to be the basis of all human action and association; but by and by, also in the wider sense that the reality which was in contradiction to these principles had, in fact, to be turned upside down" (Engels 1978, 683–84). There is an important truth lurking here—imagination and a repudiation of the present in favor of the possible is an integral part of every social upheaval.

The other form of imagination is more complicated: the inactive imagination, which makes the present absent. Kateb blasts this sort of imagination as "blindness" whereby one does not "accord full reality to everyone but oneself or one's group" and refuses to see individual activities as part of a larger reality (Kateb 2002, 501). Hence this kind of imagination is a sort of refusal to see oneself connected to others or the world—it is to have only oneself be real. Therefore, when faced with the actions of others or consequences that must be borne by others, we do not engage in empathy. Their problems are only two-dimensional and not real enough to provoke any sort of response on our own part.

Kateb brilliantly points out that the combination of the two forms of imagination is particularly disastrous. A leader armed with hyperactive imagination can use the masses blinded by their inactive imagination to create terror and misery on a virtually unlimited scale. Yet the two forms of imagination combine not just via a polity and its leader, but also in the engagement of a group identity. "I call the self-incorporation of oneself into a We a double process of using the imagination and refusing to use it. My reason is that by identifying with a group to a point of merger and self-loss, one sees oneself as everywhere present in others and everywhere absent as oneself" (497). Hence both forms of imagination combine in a single actor, and create a simultaneous narcissism and self-abnegation that has the effect of erasing the reality of the world and masking one's responsibility for it. This is an excellent hypothesis for both our paralysis in public and our search for self-identity, which fails because of our disengagement from the world. I will address this more fully in Chapter 2.

While Kateb may be right to point to these different types of imagination wreaking havoc in human lives, he overestimates the extent to which these forms are products of individual will. Kateb wants to reascribe responsibility and awareness where they have been lacking. But imagination is not entirely controlled by the individual. In fact, imagination may be an interior process that is felt to be individual, but that results from collective formations.

In *The Arcades Project,* Walter Benjamin made the following observation about the nineteenth century, but the same still holds true for the twenty-first. "The nineteenth century: singular fusion of individualistic and collectivist tendencies. Unlike virtually every previous age, it labels all actions 'individualistic' while subterraneanly, in despised everyday domains, it necessarily furnishes, as in a delirium, the elements of collective formation" (Benjamin 1999, 390). Here, Benjamin points to a paradox also noted over a century earlier by Alexis de Tocqueville (1969) about American democracy. The more individualistic a people, the less varied its culture. Tocqueville described the birth of democratic despotism in the United States; Benjamin's work explains how collective consciousness is disseminated as individual desire through consumerist phantasmagorias. We experience our collective life as fulfillment of our own, personal unconsciousness. Public life is overtaken by the fulfillment of individual fantasy, not the overcoming of individual viewpoint. It is the ability to make public life into nothing but the fulfillment of individual desire that makes us desire, and enjoy, the phantasmagoria. We can live in a collective world consisting of "individualized" dreams.

Second, the phantasmagoria is a collective spectacle that, like the fetishism of commodities, obscures the origins of its production. Is it a fantasy of self to get dressed every day, to choose a brand of juice, to drive a particular car to work? Are these individual or collective preferences? What are the markers that make our lives our own? Benjamin's brilliance comes in describing the materialist origins of collective fantasy. This brings us to the question: What *is* the material of our imagination?

The description of simultaneous narcissism and disengagement from the world is similar in Kateb's and Benjamin's work. Both describe the imagination in somewhat tragic terms. But Kateb still views the imagination as primarily individual, the content of which comes to have disastrous implications for society. Benjamin's description of the fusion of individualistic and collective desire seems incomparably bleak. Are we totally free individual agents or are we hapless puppets of collective imperatives? To say that imagination is fueled socially, but felt individually, treads a fruitful middle ground. The individual and the social are not opposing forces, but mutually informing. Imagination allows us to see this intricate process at work.

The phantasmagoria in many ways sounds like the pinnacle of totalitarianism, all the more terrifying because it is felt as our own impulses. But let us consider an alternative depiction of the imagination at work offered by Benjamin. The phantasmagoria encourages unconsciousness while we are awake—the dreamworld is, quite literally, the consciousness that is available to us when we are asleep. Benjamin writes of dream eras and dream cities in order to emphasize the physical act of sleeping—we sleep in particular locations, and each era contains the sleeping of its inhabitants. He repeatedly refers to subterranean dreams, implying that they are both earthly and somehow beneath the social activities of the day. I want to emphasize, however, that dreams are not an alternative reality—they, like the phantasmagoria, are already implicated in the world as it is. There is no "outside" of the social order, only that which is represented to us as outside. We cannot fantasize or dream our way outside of our reality, no matter how complete our phantasmagorias become. The present economic and cultural reality conditions our dreaming "precisely as, with the sleeper, an overfull stomach finds not its reflection but its expression in the contents of dreams" (Benjamin 1999, 392). We do not dream of having a full stomach, but a full stomach changes and colors our dreams. Similarly, we do not dream of the world order, of consumer capitalism, but it nonetheless governs our dreams.

In dreaming we express our world, our reality. "The collective from the first, expresses the conditions of its life. These find their expression in the dream and their reinterpretation in the awakening" (392). The conditions of our existence are expressed in our dreams. Then, as we wake up and move from one state of consciousness to another, the chance of fresh realization is present. We can see things in a new way: our dreams may tell us when we are unhappy and refuse to admit it to ourselves, or may provide the solution to a problem that we cannot acknowledge while awake. Benjamin asserts, "The realization of dream elements, in the course of waking up, is the paradigm of dialectical thinking" (13). We can achieve a distance from what *is* through different states of consciousness and modes of interpretation. This interplay of perspective on the world and our place within it is the origin of dialectical thinking about our social existence, not a space outside of it. The role of the intellectual, then, is to help develop awareness of this movement between dreaming and imagination and the material conditions that influence them. How exactly are dreams of community influenced and shaped by liberal individualism and capitalism?

I prefer Benjamin's understanding of imagination because it tells us how our particular eras compel us to particular forms and ways of imagining. Kateb's description of our imagining is apt, yet it cannot explain why the forms of imagination he delineates have become predominant in the twentieth century. Kateb's individual imagination holds out promise that the right kind of imagination will create the right kind of politics, yet it is difficult for me to see how this is substantially different from the hyperactive imagination that he describes. It seems that imagination needs to be understood as the connection between individual and collective. In this way, the individual is influenced by the collective, yet this also holds out the possibility that the individual may come to influence the collective in return. It is when the dynamic relationship between the two, individual and collective, becomes unidirectional that the relationship becomes troubling. Both Kateb and Benjamin point to this problem in their work: when Kateb's individual loses the world or dominates it, distortion occurs. Similarly, when Benjamin's phantasmagoria infuses both our intimate and public experiences to the exclusion of all else, resistance becomes inconceivable. Imagination should not be understood as only collective or entirely individual, it is the interplay of the two elements that distinguishes it.

I have been describing the interaction between individual and collective in imagination, I now want to turn to my other axis, the question of how imagination relates to both theory and practice. Once again, if we conceptualize imagination allied with one end of the spectrum rather than the other, the political potential of imagination becomes lost. Consider the consequences for action if we too firmly align ideals of community with theory. If community is understood as entirely separate from, and opposed to, the given social and political circumstances of our time this leads to a potentially dangerous dynamic. For if community is viewed as unrelated to what we have, the most apparent way of using community as critique is to use it to deny or criticize the existing reality. In this way, the ideal, community, is used to denigrate the material, liberal capitalism. This can lead to a particularly stale form of criticism that may actually impede action.

For example, Julia Kristeva asserts that "feminist practice can only be negative, at odds with what already exists so that we may say 'that's not it' and 'that's still not it'" (Kristeva 1980, 137). Because we cannot know what women would be in a world that was not patriarchal, we cannot speak from an affirmative position. Therefore, political potential is restricted to a denunciation of the present. Similarly, if we consider community as the opposite of what exists, it would be easy to fall into this kind of "negative practice." We cannot know how we would understand ourselves if we lived in a truly communal world, all we can say is that this form of social organization is not it. But this simply rejects the real in favor of an unachievable ideal. This is not a dynamic relationship where one can see how ideal and material are interconnected and mutually constituting. Without this relationship, the ideal cannot serve to change the real, it can only deny it, over and over again.

THE UNMOORED IMAGINATION

Yet there *is* a problem with imagining community in a world governed by liberal individualism. On what grounds can you base your imagination? How is it possible to imagine a community or a public if you don't live in one? Hannah Arendt points out the difficulty of political imagination in *Men in Dark Times: Thoughts on Lessing* (Arendt 1968). To achieve a renunciation of the current political order, the most common method is to engage in what Arendt calls "the inner migration." Those who see themselves at odds with the current world order, or who are seen by the world order as at odds with itself, are tempted to retract from the world. Nietzsche describes the stifling of possibility in the world that leads people to develop inwards as the birth of the soul (Nietzsche 1989, 84–85). Yet Arendt cautions against this tendency. "But seductive though it may be to yield to such temptations and to hole up in the refuge of one's own psyche, the result will always be a loss of humanness along with a forsaking of reality" (Arendt 1968, 23). Arendt describes eras of history when through either discrimination or lack of freedom, thinkers have not been able to exist within a public sphere. Although they feel that they have gained freedom through their withdrawal, sociality is what characterizes the human condition—to sacrifice this aspect of worldly existence is to sacrifice humanity.

When we dismiss collective life as illusory, the implication is that there must be something "more real" somewhere else, or even underneath it. To find this space, we retreat in what Arendt termed an interior migration—we become locked into our own minds, try to ignore the larger world, which is false anyway, and instead build ever more inclusive private spaces to reflect, to save ourselves. "When men are deprived of the public space—they retreat into their freedom of thought" (9). Arendt points out that these interior spaces lose meaning when not counterbalanced through collective engagement. When we cannot or will not orient ourselves with others, we lose any associational reference point. Ultimately, our interior space of freedom evolves into a real worldlessness, an inability to be in the world. The ability to distinguish what is phantom and what is real becomes even more difficult, and hence we start to contribute to the irreality of the world, rather than merely avoiding it.

Furthermore, we then abandon collective experience to phantoms. Adopting Arendt's definition, the world is "the thing that arises between people and in which everything that individuals carry with them innately can become visible and audible" (10). If phantoms govern collective experience, there is no world outside the phantasmagoria. The phantasmagoria is also singular in its collectivity—it provides the scripted comfort that we seek. Collectivity becomes singular, which is what Arendt believes is the supreme danger in politics: If "all men would suddenly unite in a single opinion . . . the world, which can form only in the interspaces between men in all their variety, would vanish altogether" (31). Here we return to Benjamin's definition of modernity—it is the world overtaken by its phantasmagorias. It is *this* reality that we must awaken to, not some other, clearer, more straightforward, moral world that lurks under our circus of appearance. When we revert back to the opposition of truth and illusion, recognition of illusion allows us to distance ourselves from it. Instead we must awaken to our collective sleeping; it is this passing consciousness within the phantasmagoria itself that will provide new dreams to be realized.

Imagination is central in political life, both in creating revolution and in maintaining order. For this reason, I assert that it is crucial to look at our dreams of community, and political imagination in general, as vacillating between individual and collective, theory and material. The dialectical tension that is manifest when we see our dreams of community as responding to already existing conditions will help us to see more clearly what can be done. On the other hand, we also need to see how our imagination is limited. When it becomes too disconnected from the world, it fails to create change. When it becomes trained and adopts too many assumptions of the present order, it fails to provide an alternative one. Finally, when the world captures political imagination, it can lose the power of individual freedom. In the chapters that follow, I will explore each of these problems by looking at ideas of community in contemporary politics.

2

A ROOM FULL OF MIRRORS
Community and the Promise of Identity

> We cannot give a proper account of ourselves. We cannot sit together and tell comprehensible stories, and we recognize ourselves in the stories we read only when these are fragmented narratives, without plots, the literary equivalent of atonal music and nonrepresentational art.
> —MICHAEL WALZER, "THE COMMUNITARIAN CRITIQUE OF LIBERALISM"

Classical liberalism took individual identity as a given: first there were individuals, then these individuals formed society. There have been critics of this claim for as long as it has been made. For example, Rousseau described how the individual fundamentally changes with the establishment of society. Identity, originally a function of independence and an inner sense of self (amour soi), becomes a function of artifice and the presentation of self to others (amour propre). To some extent, this original sense of self is no longer recoverable. Rousseau cautions, "Let us therefore take care not to confuse savage man with the men we have before our eyes" (Rousseau 1964, 111). Hegel goes one step further and argues that self-consciousness does not become perverted by society, but can only occur as a result of it: "But in point of fact self-consciousness is the reflection out of the being of the world of sense and perception, and is essentially the return from otherness" (Hegel 1977, 105).

The social constitution of identity has become one of the most predominant critiques of liberalism's a priori assumption of the individual. The observation that selves reflect and are brought into effect by their environments is a claim that very few would dispute at this point, and even prominent liberal theorists have incorporated this understanding into their theories. Since the individual is the sun around which our society revolves, it makes sense that we exhibit a fascination with the social interactions that constitute modern selves.

But if the notion of socially constituted identities is now widely accepted, the political ramifications of this process are still under debate. In one prominent version of the story of identity formation, theorists emphasize the oppositional nature of identity construction in Hegelian dialectics, where a self develops in relationship to "the other." It is through the logic of exclusion, creating boundaries, and developing oppositional identity categories that the material of self is supplied socially. In another rendition, talking about socially constituted subjects can also sound as though individuals are putty in the hands of a churning mechanism that places people in previously established "subject positions." Foucault described the role of social structures as "forc[ing] the individual back on himself and ties him to his own identity in a constraining way" (Foucault 1984, 173). The development of individual identity through membership in a "community" has emerged as a preferable alternative to these two options.

Theorists have begun to look at communities as an integral element in developing a positive individual identity (Weir 1996). For some time, it was a trope that the "true" individual somehow stood apart from, or even developed in resistance to, his or her community; individualism and membership were seen as diametrically opposed. Today, rather than individuals being at odds with community, it is assumed that individuals need communal membership to recognize and develop themselves as such. For example, Shane Phelan, who writes about lesbian feminist politics, is suspicious of the concept of community because it may act as a homogenizing force. Nonetheless, she claims, "The construction of a positive identity requires a community that supports that identity" (Phelan 1989, 59). Lisa Tessman has also declared, "It is a mistake to think that one could maintain a desired identity (as a living, changing identity) apart from the community/communities that sustain it" (Tessman 1995, 64). One of the most appealing aspects of the common understanding of community today is that it delivers socially constituted identities without a loss of freedom and without coercion. Communities are where we can choose membership and have our selves reflected back or recognized in a favorable light.

The resurgence of interest in community is linked to the awareness of the politics of identity construction in the United States in the 1980s and early 1990s. This linkage between identity construction and community has created some rather strange bedfellows in my discussion of identity and community. In the early 1980s, activists started to talk about the importance of community in creating more positive connotations for previously disenfranchised groups, such as women and racial and sexual minorities (Reagon

1983; Lorde 1984). At this point, the exclusive nature of identity formation was emphasized, different identities were stigmatized, and others were valorized through the process of exclusion. In response, strengthening communities where previously marginalized groups could be "insiders" was a primary political goal. But as the theory of socially influenced identity construction became more prevalent, and perhaps as a reaction to identity politics movements of the 1980s, soon groups who did not have marginalized identities also began to talk about identity and community. After all, it is not just through exclusion that identity is formed, but also through inclusion.

Richard Ford noted that in many ways, communitarianism was like identity politics for white men (1995). Amy Gutmann's essay, "The Communitarian Critics of Liberalism," noted that an emphasis upon identity is what distinguishes the so-called New Communitarians from a long tradition of communitarian philosophy. Gutmann claims that communitarianism was once driven by the ideas of Marx, with an emphasis upon collective ownership and community self-determination. (I would add that the Republican tradition of the common good and citizenship are missing from Gutmann's characterization.) Conversely, New Communitarians are highly influenced by Hegelian thought. "The Hegelian conception of man as a historically conditioned being" (Gutmann 1992, 121) forms the core of the New Communitarian critique of democratic liberalism. And Gutmann's most recent book, *Identity in Democracy*, contests the opposition between identity politics and interest-based politics, asserting that "one of the neglected issues that identity group politics therefore poses for democratic society is the way in which recognition of interests often follows from group identification rather than being given simply by the pre-existing interests of individuals apart from their group identification" (Gutmann 2003, 14). That such a claim would appear in the work of a staunch liberal is a marker of the achievements of theorists of difference who chipped away at the assumption of an abstract individual, as well as of ontological communitarians such as Michael Sandel, who argued that it was impossible to see individuals as separate from their social contexts.

In terms of political history, it is tempting to trace whether or not the adoption of the theory and language of identity politics by the mainstream in American politics can be dismissed as a case of counterhegemonic cooptation. After all, one might ask whether identity politics was revolutionary if its basic assumptions were adopted by the dominant groups in society. While it is impossible to definitively answer such a question, I do believe that there are instructive contrasts to be drawn between these different groups, hence my juxtaposition of the ideas of such disparate thinkers. This discussion highlights that all of these varied thinkers have adopted the predominant interpretation of Hegel's master-slave dialectic. I believe that considering his alternative resolution for the battle to achieve self-recognition can offer a way out of the dilemma above and can revolutionize our understanding of the relationship between identity, community, and politics once more.

HEGEL'S MASTER-SLAVE DIALECTIC: TWO RESOLUTIONS

While it seems that the importance of identity to politics and its status as a social construction have been established, there is still disagreement about how to understand the power dynamics of these processes. The problem is that developing self-consciousness has not been predominantly envisioned as a mutually beneficial or even particularly respectful enterprise. Now that identity construction is widely perceived to be an integral aspect of contemporary politics, it becomes more pressing to conceptualize ways to minimize its inegalitarianism. Historically, identity construction has been viewed as a key component of political oppression, not to mention an enterprise that is more frequently thwarted than one that can be understood as given. Hegel's exploration of the relationship between master and slave creates the paradigmatic understanding of identity formation. "Self-consciousness is faced by another self-consciousness; it has come out of itself. This has a two fold significance; first it has lost itself, for it finds itself as an other being; secondly, in doing so it has superseded the other, for it does not see the other as an essential being, but in the other sees its own self" (Hegel 1977, 111). Here Hegel unveils the paradoxical and ultimately self-defeating dynamic of creating self-consciousness. To find oneself, one must leave oneself. But every self naturally sees itself as immediate, it cannot truly recognize others as independent entities without extensive prodding. Instead, the self only sees others in inverse relation—they are "not-I's" rather than genuinely independent others. This narcissism ultimately frustrates the search for self-recognition because "self-consciousness achieves its satisfaction only in another self-consciousness" (110). If we cannot recognize the other as an independent self, then, in turn, that other cannot provide the recognition that we seek.

It is this dynamic that was fully explicated in gender and racial theory of the twentieth century, most notably in the work of Simone de Beauvoir (1953) and Frantz Fanon (1967). We have come to see this process in social relations characterized by inequality between races, in the opposition of heterosexuality and homosexuality, and that between masculinity and femininity. But it is important to remember that the same dynamic holds even in cases without clearly evident inequalities.

Hegel offers two potential solutions to this dilemma. In the first version, the slave, through labor and the stifling of his own desires, "becomes conscious of what he truly is" (Hegel 1977, 118). The slave, whose imagined self finds no referent in the outside world, is forced to recognize the limitations of his self-consciousness. If his sense of self finds no reflection in his environment, he is forced to recognize the impotence of his consciousness. Instead, he gains a less distorted image of self that is based upon his material interaction with the world, his labor. Hence, through the denial of his desired self, he arrives at a true recognition of self vis-à-vis his connection with the world. Hegel emphasizes that it is through interaction with the world that we can achieve a true recognition of ourselves.

The other solution enjoys more predominance today. (After all, who wants to embrace the role of the oppressed in self-discovery through labor?) The second strategy begins with the master, and his overcoming his own power to achieve true recognition with the slave. In contrast to the slave, Hegel's master, enjoying all the advantages of power, is able to control the world and manipulate it to his own ends. Nevertheless, his process of coming to self-consciousness is frustrated. His power enables him to maintain the illusion of omnipotence and self in a way that the slave cannot. This is a crucial and frequently forgotten element of Hegel's analysis. We are inclined to see the world as a reflection of ourselves, and power helps to maintain this illusion. Because we can only achieve self-consciousness through an experience of the world as separate from self, power can actually impede the development of true self-consciousness. In seeing the slave and in experiencing the world as a mere appendage, the master's search is frustrated since he cannot obtain independent confirmation of his identity. Instead, a master has the illusion of identity, as the world is filtered by his imagination to serve the fantasy of self.

Regardless of his power, ultimately the master's need for independent confirmation of his identity wins out. First he needs to have independent selves recognize him. Second, the illusion of total control of another being is fragile and cannot be sustained. The slave is revealed to be independent of his master's desires. Both of these factors combine to create a situation where master and slave see each other as independent entities. Through this recognition of mutual independence, they are able to recognize each other.

The key to both resolutions is that the failure of the world and other people to conform to our desires forces the individual to recognize the bounded nature of his or her self-consciousness. While we naturally place ourselves at the center of the world and see everything through our own thick lens, eventually we are compelled to acknowledge that the world does not exist in a subservient relationship to our imagination.

Once the illusion of total omnipotence is broken, master and slave recognize one another as selves, and hence the universality of selfhood is the method by which particularity is also revealed. Mutual recognition delivers individual identity through the acknowledgement of the "we." The problem of the "other" (or "not-I") is solved through the creation, or recognition, of a "we."

This reading of Hegel demonstrates a number of important points. First, it becomes clear why so many theorists are currently drawn to the possibilities of community. In one formulation, communities are where those who were or are "others" in the society at large can find a positive rather than negative identity. In another vision, communities are where the universal "we" of humanity can transcend politicized identities and create solidarity. This explains why both theorists who value "difference" and those who look for solidarity or universality embrace community as a central component of their political visions. In this chapter, I will explore how theorists of difference and hybridity, as well as theorists who embrace universalism, emphasize this second reading of Hegel's solution to the master-slave dialectic.

Yet Hegel's dialectic also demonstrates something about imagination and politics. In Hegel's description, the slave is favored in the process of achieving self-recognition because his imagination has a more limited power. The master, whose illusions are sustained for longer through his formidable power, is slower (and perhaps ultimately unable) to come to consciousness of the universal, and, consequently, of himself. The inability to find a self occurs when the dialectical tension between self and other fails, but also when the creative interaction between self as imagined and the phenomenal situation in which this imagination seeks to realize itself collapses. Paradoxically, the more power enables the imagination, the less it is able to realize itself. When community is offered as the resolution to the struggle between self and world in identity construction, it privileges the individual imagination at the cost of the world and also the self. This discussion will return to Hegel's alternative resolution of the master-slave dialectic below, and suggest ways that this may influence the way we think about identity in contemporary politics.

COMMUNITY AND SELF/SELVES

As I have established, both theorists who embrace universal humanism and those who value difference have come to see community as the key to their respective political visions. The following discussion will demonstrate how community comes to be the term of intersection between the proclaimed aporia of universalism and difference. While theorists such as Charles Taylor and Philip Selznick position themselves in opposition to theorists of identity politics, a close reading reveals that many of their ideas about identity and community are quite similar.

In *The Ethics of Authenticity*, Charles Taylor applies his understanding of Hegel to an analysis of identity politics (Taylor 1975). He argues that identity politics groups wrongly claim that their alienation stems from the stigma attached to their identity or the failure of the dominant culture to recognize it on equal terms. Taylor argues that the "belief in authenticity," not inequality, is really to blame for alienation. He describes the logic of authenticity as a belief that the truth does not exist in the outside world; it can only be found inside oneself. Consequently, morality must also be found within, and this is what many believe it means to be a self-legislating subject. Therefore, freedom, morality, and finding one's identity become inextricably connected in the ideal of authenticity.

Taylor persuasively argues that this belief in authenticity has led to an irresolvable dilemma in contemporary society. Our idea of an authentic self is that we have an inner core that exists apart from all outside influence. Yet discovering who we are requires that we acquire "a language of self-definition." "A language only exists and is maintained within a language community. And this indicates another crucial feature of the self. One is a self only among other selves. A self can never be described without reference to those who surround it" (Taylor 1989, 35). By claiming that we must separate ourselves from the world to discover who we are, the ideal of authenticity robs us of our tools of self-definition. Taylor argues that our identities are formed out of moral frameworks in relationship to our concept of the good: "Otherwise put, I can define my identity only against the background of things that matter. But to bracket out history, nature, society, the demands of solidarity, everything but what I find in myself, would be to eliminate all candidates for what matters" (Taylor 1992, 40–41). We may define ourselves, but we must do so with the tools that are provided by society—namely, language—and in relationship to goods that exist outside of ourselves as well. The belief in authenticity, by separating us from others and larger moral frameworks, effectively makes it impossible to discover "who we really are." The parallel with the self-defeating consciousness of Hegel's description is quite clear.

Taylor asserts that identity groups, led by the belief in authenticity, emphasize difference at the cost of community. For example, he assumes that "the politics of recognition" is concerned with the recognition of difference in a fetishistic manner, a sort of cult of uniqueness. This insistence on singularity echoes Hegel's master, who tries to prove his own unique position by denying his connection to the slave. The struggle for recognition in identity politics is, according to Taylor, still a struggle between self-consciousness and consciousness. By demanding that others recognize their difference, groups overtly based upon identity continue to repeat the master's initial mistake. Resolution can only occur when one group stops asserting its subjectivity at the cost of any other's.

Just as the master-slave dialectic ends through recognition of mutuality, identity politics struggles can only be resolved by realizing a universal human community. For now, groups push others to acknowledge and honor their difference. However, Taylor points out that "mere difference can't itself be the ground of equal value" (51). He responds by claiming that recognition of difference also requires recognition of similarity. Identity politics groups deny connection to others and common humanity in the interest of demanding recognition for their unique identity. In other words, Taylor's analysis implies that groups based upon identity are attempting to occupy the role of master in the contemporary manifestation of the master-slave dialectic.

Taylor offers a solution to the dilemma created by this belief in authenticity. He reconciles the fact that we are socially conditioned beings with the desire to be self-legislating by asserting that there is no difference between who we are and what surrounds us. Hegel calls this condition of perfect harmony "infinity": "a condition in which the subject is not limited by anything outside" (Taylor 1975, 148). Taylor calls this recognition of similarity "community." The public world has become more individualized, thus requiring that we experience "a stronger, more inner sense of linkage" in order to realize that we are part of a "wider whole" (Taylor 1992, 91). Recognizing similarities between ourselves and others, and being part of this "wider whole," is Taylor's description of "genuine authenticity." Our search for self ends with the recognition of similarity, of universality, of community.

Some problems with Taylor's theory of identity can be explored by juxtaposing his analysis with feminist critiques of the concept of community and the process of identity formation. Such a comparison illustrates first that Taylor's idea of having an environment reflect the self is a privilege, not a given condition. Second, it presents the question, how is it possible to have a unified subject that is constructed by relating to a heterogeneous world?

Taylor's belief in homogeneity is never directly approached by Maria Lugones, yet a close reading of his theory reveals what she terms "the logic of purity." Lugones contrasts two different ways of seeing the world: one is driven by the need for purity, the other embraces multiplicity. Lugones states that the fundamental assumption of the logic of purity is that "There is unity underlying multiplicity" (Lugones 1994, 463). Social ordering follows this logic, placing people into different categories, yet inside one overall framework. Lugones describes the world view of purity as follows:

> *According to the logic of purity, the social world is both unified and fragmented, homogeneous, hierarchically ordered. Each person is either fragmented, composite, or abstract and unified—not exclusive alternatives. Unification and homogeneity are related principles of ordering the social world. Unification requires a fragmented and hierarchical ordering. Fragmentation is another guise of unity, both in the collectivity and the individual.* (463)[1]

In other words, Lugones defines purity as the need for unity or homogeneity. In order to provide for homogeneity in a world that is resolutely heterogeneous, we can divide people, characteristics, and categories into a dichotomous order. Each of these groups remains homogeneous and the categories are established as neat oppositions that rest upon the same spectrum.

Taylor reveals this tendency toward purity when he asserts that there is no way that one community can really reflect an individual. Instead, she must belong to several communities in order to have all of her self "revealed." Embracing a complex, even contradictory, identity means that membership in multiple communities comes to be an essential part of having freedom of identity. Taylor describes multiple memberships as follows:

> The full definition of someone's identity thus usually involves not only his stand on moral and spiritual matters but also some

---

1. Lugones "speaks" in two different voices throughout the text (Lugones 1994); the italics here appear in the original material and indicate one of those two voices.

> reference to a defining community. These two dimensions were reflected in the examples which quite naturally came to mind in my discussion above, where I spoke of identifying oneself as a Catholic or an anarchist, or as an Armenian or a Québecois. *Normally, however, one dimension would not be exclusive of the other.* Thus it might be essential to the self-definition of A that he is a Catholic and a Québecois; of B that he is an Armenian and an anarchist. (And these descriptions might not exhaust the identity of either.) (Taylor 1989, 36)

Taylor's conception of multiple memberships fails to account for community memberships that pull us in different directions every day, such as commitments to both family life and a career. Being an exemplary member of a family may be diametrically opposed to what it takes to be a model employee. Or consider the struggle of being the first openly gay Episcopal bishop. If our identity is socially constituted in both of these realms, how does one negotiate often contradictory demands?

And what are the ramifications of saying that one needs multiple communities to reflect different aspects of oneself? Multiple memberships rescue the idea of homogeneous communities. Communities only need to reflect a given attribute, the same one, in all of their members. Any other aspect of a person's identity can be reflected elsewhere. For example, how would a Catholic lesbian find a community to reflect her identity? Taylor's solution seems to be that she could belong to a Catholic parish as well as a lesbian organization. This approach rescues the purity of the different communities, since the Catholic Church need not recognize the existence of gay members, and the lesbian group need not acknowledge the presence of Catholicism in its ranks. But this solution does not necessarily give the woman a community that reflects herself. Instead, she may feel marginalized in both communities.

Although Taylor posits that communities are naturally unified, Audre Lorde's work clearly demonstrates how homogeneity in communities is maintained, most frequently through a combination of coercion and exclusion. Lorde points out that uniformity among members of a community requires that some "parts" are altered to fit the "whole" while others may be discarded altogether. First, she notes the need for solidarity among the disenfranchised group. "Historically, difference had been used so cruelly against us that as a people we were reluctant to tolerate any diversion from what was externally defined as Blackness" (Lorde 1984, 136). She points out that this imperative is not limited to racially defined groups. Women's groups are also prone to this dynamic: "By and large within the women's movement today, white women focus upon their oppression as women and ignore differences of race, sexual preference, class and age. There is a pretense to a homogeneity of experience covered by the word *sisterhood* that does not in fact exist" (116). Lorde's words serve as a reminder that a common, collective identity is not something that is passively found, but rather negotiated and created. And these negotiations may create a greater level of comfort for some members than for others.

Lugones's and Lorde's analyses point out that the harmony between personal and collective identity that Taylor assumes is actually a political process. Once we discard the myth of a natural affinity between one's self and one's community, the dynamics of building consensus become much clearer. There is no inherent correspondence between an identity and a community. Instead, the boundaries of the community must be maintained in order to create the illusion of an essential identity. Homogeneity within the community is a construct used to reinforce the myth of the identity. However, this seemingly tight circle of identification between community and member is actually dependent upon the exclusion of others—the creation of a boundary.

Bernice Johnson Reagon's speech, "Coalition Politics: Turning the Century," offers some idea of how the desire to have a surrounding that reflects oneself is manifested. Her speech is worth quoting at some length because it offers an unusually clear vision of what drives people to search for community as a source of liberation.

> The people running the society call the shots as if they're still living in one of those little villages, where they kill the ones they don't like or put them in the forest to die.... When somebody else is running a society like that, and you are the one who would be put out to die, it gets too hard to stay out in that society all the time. And that's when you find a place, and you try to bar the door and check all the people who come in. You come together to see what you can do about shouldering up all of your energies so that you and your kind can survive.... But that space while it lasts should be a nurturing space where you sift out what people are saying about you and decide who you really are. And you take the time to construct within yourself and within your community who you would be if you were running society. In fact, in that little barred

room where you check everybody at the door, you act out community. (Reagon 1983, 357–58)

It is crucial to acknowledge that, in all likelihood, there is not a place where identity is uncontested, or even comfortable. Reagon's speech recognizes this fact, as she makes clear that what happens in this safe room is "acting community." There is no actual community where transparency between self and collective exists; one can only pretend this is the case in certain bounded places and situations. The amount of material and social power held by those who belong to the collective determines how large that community is and to what extent it can insulate its members from society at large. While power assists the imagination to generate and maintain community, the imagination alone cannot deliver identity.

Some more conservative communitarians have betrayed a degree of awareness of the logic of exclusion and reinforcement of communal identity. Perhaps they do so unconsciously, as these same theorists clearly state that they embrace heterogeneous communities. For example, in "A Moderate Communitarian Proposal" Amitai Etzioni defends against the charge of liberal thinkers that deriving personal identity from communal membership is a form of totalitarianism. Suddenly, the unified self that is the product of membership in a homogeneous community disappears. Instead, Etzioni offers a surprisingly frenetic vision: "The uncommunitized personhood is a source of creativity and change for the community and fulfillment for the person. The communitized part of the person is a source of service for shared needs and a source of stability and support for social virtues of the community" (Etzioni 1996b, 157). Benjamin Barber makes a similar distinction between "the individual" and "the citizen" inside us all in his introduction to *Strong Democracy* (Barber 1984, xv). Both thinkers suggest that a core self, independent of social influence, will persist in the context of community. These configurations offer a fascinating alternative to drawing the boundaries of a community to exclude some people. Instead, the boundary of a community, and the meaning of membership in it, can be delineated by drawing the boundary *inside oneself*. This is one way of substantiating the communitarian claim that membership in their communities is inclusive—apparently inclusive only of particular fragments of the self.

Barber's and Etzioni's solutions to the problem of individual freedom have only created a more fragmentary vision of self. They may have reconciled the notion of freedom in the face of the social constitution of identity, but they have done so at the cost of any kind of coherence whatsoever. Struggling for dialogue between the "uncommunitized" and "communitized" aspects of self, or the "citizen" and "individual," leads to a considerably more complicated vision of personal identity than they started with. Maria Lugones's reflections on purity are relevant again here. She has observed how the need for purity, by dissecting different aspects of our identity, naturally creates a fragmented rather than unified self. "So, for example, the multiplicitous beings required for the production of a unified subject are anomalous as multiple. Unity renders them anomalous. So they are altered to fit within the logic of unification. They are split over and over in accordance with the relevant dichotomies of the logic of unity" (Lugones 1994, 468). Multiple memberships that allow us to feel like there is a community that supports every different, particular aspect of our identities lead to more and more splintering and confusion. Lugones points out that trying to find reflections of our selves in a fragmented society leads to fragmented identities and an even more polarized social landscape:

> Social homogeneity, domination through unification, and hierarchical ordering of split social groups are connected tightly to fragmentation in the person. If the person is fragmented, it is because the society is itself fragmented into groups that are pure, homogeneous. Each group's structure of affiliation to and through transparent members produces a society of persons who are fragmented as they are affiliated to separate groups. As the parts of the individuals are separate, the groups are separate, in an insidious dialectic. (475)

Our selves become increasing fragmented as we are compartmentalized in order to accommodate the logic of purity. Maintaining this purity requires that groups also maintain their distinctness from one another.

Of course, neither society nor personal understanding of self is static and this fact has created anxiety among a number of communitarian thinkers. Although the communitarian emphasis is upon the instability of community in the contemporary world, a fear for the stability of self is also evident in some work. Amitai Etzioni observes that "when community (social webs carrying moral values) breaks down, the individual's psychological integrity is endangered" (Etzioni 1995, 16). Similarly, Philip Selznick proposes, "The findings of modern social science confirm the need for a stabilizing center in human life. For such a center to exist, there must be psychic autonomy within a framework of bonding to other persons and to person-centered activities. Such a self is not free-floating: it emerges from and is sustained by specific personal relationships. Only in and through such bonds—only if there is an embedded self—will the center hold" (Selznick 1995, 110). The "center" to which Selznick refers in this passage is ambiguous. Is it the community that reinforces the embedded self? Or is it the self that is threatened? By conflating a stable self with the community that sustains and creates it, these passages reveal that hidden under the desire for community may be a desire for a unified self. This self is threatened not only by the social constitution of identity, but also by the desire to make inclusive communities that are universally valid.

COMMUNITIES OF DIFFERENCE AND THE DISSOLUTION OF SELF

From the previous discussion it is evident that trying to reconcile free choice and community membership stretches the subject in many directions—eventually resulting in a split. Although Taylor tries to deal with this split by advocating multiple memberships, the fragmented subject continues to haunt communitarian descriptions of identity formation. Those familiar with debates in feminist theory over the past fifteen years know that feminist theorists have directly grappled with the problems of community and identity formation (Alcoff 1988). Was assuming a category of women an ascriptive, oppressive gesture, or was women's community the instrument of self-definition? Recent feminist theorists have argued that relinquishing the idea of a unified subject will overcome the need of homogenization, or, as Lugones calls it, "the logic of purity." In this regard, they seem to be following the lead of Luce Irigaray, who believes that women have been positioned as men's reflection. Woman is merely the repository for the penis, a "not-male" that is singular in its nonidentity. Female subjectivity is assumed to be singular because it is an inversion of male subjectivity, predicated upon the singular phallus.

> Let's leave one to them: their oneness, with its prerogatives, its domination, its solipsism: like the sun's. And the strange way they divide up their couples, with the other as the image of the one. Only an image. So any move toward the other means turning back to the attraction of one's mirage. A (scarcely) living mirror, she/it is frozen, mute. More lifelike. The ebb and flow of our lives spent

in the exhausting labor of copying, miming. Dedicated to reproducing—that sameness in which we have remained for centuries, as the other. (Irigaray 1985, 207)

Irigaray points out that female sexual organs are multiple, neither one, nor even two (28). She intends to implode the logic of reflection by pointing out female multiplicity. In order to free themselves from being "a (scarcely) living mirror" women must embrace their multiplicity. Recognition of multiple subjectivity is one path toward recovering one's own self, of breaking through the looking glass. The attempt to construct an unnaturally unified self leads to social atomization and discrimination, creating the conjunction of liberal individualist ontology and racial and sexual subordination. The best way to overcome this dynamic is to embrace multiplicitous selves.

Irigaray's insight has been more fully explored by postcolonial feminists who share her interest in interrupting the assumptions of a unified, standard femaleness in order to recognize both gender and racial differentiation. However, it seems even theories of multiple subjectivities do not escape the logic of the mirror between selves and community.

Trinh T. Minh-Ha's work is a valuable reverie on the logic of identity and offers a more complicated picture of the way that "essentialized" identity actually works. First, as I have already noted, membership in the community is limited in order to preserve the fiction of the essential, or given, identity of its members. Limiting membership is a way to make homogeneity look automatic. Consequently, "Any attempts at blurring the dividing line between outsider and insider would justifiably cause anxiety, if not anger" (Trinh 1989, 70).

Taylor dismisses the subordination of the master-slave dialectic as a temporary stage of identity construction, but Trinh aptly observes that these relationships of domination have become the primary forum for identity development. "One's sense of self is always mediated by the image one has of the other. (I have asked myself at times whether a superficial knowledge of the other, in terms of some stereotype, is not a way of preserving a superficial image of oneself.)" (73). She is pointing out that the master may assert her identity through the body of the slave, or other. Paradoxically, this superficial view of the other allows the master to avoid knowing herself. Taylor hypothesizes that individualism and the belief in authenticity prevents self-knowledge. Trinh points out that in actuality it is relationships characterized by domination, not isolation, that keep us from engaging in a process of self-discovery. Furthermore, her reading prompts us to question whether the search for recognition is indeed stronger than the desire to dominate. Would we relinquish fantasies of omnipotence in favor of more accurate conceptions of self?

Trinh also rejects the idea of recognizing unity as the solution to the dilemma of self-other. Instead, she moves beyond the critique of an essentialized identity to question unified identity as well. "For there can hardly be such a thing as an essential inside that can be homogeneously represented by all insiders; an authentic insider in there, an absolute reality out there, or an incorrupted representative who cannot be questioned by another incorrupted representative" (75). She discards the promise of community, stating that there is no place where we may be reflected in our entirety. This is because "differences do not exist between outsider and insider—two entities—they are also at work within the outsider or the insider—a single entity" (76). In other words, difference in communities reflects differences within ourselves. In order to break out of the relationship of domination so aptly described in Hegel's master-slave dialectic, we need to embrace multiple selves and communities of difference.

These reflections upon the linkages between community and the problem of difference are discussed by Lisa Tessman. She attempts to show how communities can overcome a "unity" constructed either through exclusion of membership or exclusion of characteristics in its membership, or both. She writes, "I envision a process where within any collectivity we aim to remake ourselves in the direction of hybridity, for it is a hybrid self that will develop when the meanings of the collectivity in which our identities are forming are contested" (Tessman 1995, 79). And furthermore, "This remaking of ourselves in the coalition community does not decrease our differences; rather, it increases the degree of hybridity within all of us" (80). Tessman's agonistic communities will allow everyone to develop a number of selves. The multiplication of personal identity will make it impossible to maintain boundaries or exclude someone based upon a shared characteristic in the community. Furthermore, these agonistic communities will provide a more accurate and comfortable reflection of our truly multiple selves.

Tessman tries to articulate an alternative vision of community, one that fosters multiple selves. Theoretically, this is the most comfortable position for a liberatory politics that includes a notion of community. There is no exclusion, because communities themselves are not driven by a need for coherence. There is no anguish over identity characteristics that seem contradictory, because the self is not understood as a singular entity. The mélange of self/selves is reflected and endorsed by the chaotic communities that surround it/them.

But this solution to the need for inclusion actually falls into the same dynamic as the pursuit for a unified identity. After all, the same reflective dynamic is present between a homogeneous community and a unified self that exists between a diverse community and a multiplicitous self. In the basic sense, the vision of fragmented community is still driven by the need to rescue and stroke the self or selves as it or they are imagined. Tessman values communities of difference to reflect one's natural heterogeneity. Lugones states, "*I realize that separation into clean, tidy things and beings is not possible for me because it would be the death of myself as multiplicitous and a death of community with my own*" (Lugones 1994, 469). In Lugones's view, the logic of purity tries to separate hybrid communities and rob people with multiple selves of a natural community. For both, rejecting the logic of purity allows everyone to establish a reflective identity between self and community.

The central theme articulated by all of these theorists is the need to have community mirror oneself. The dialectical relationship between imagination and the world is thereby short-circuited. In such a schema, imagination inevitably seeks to shape circumstances to serve itself. Yet this exercise of imagination, as Hegel so eloquently described, hinders our experience of the world and recognition of other people, as well our recognition of ourselves. Whether the self is idealized as unified or multiple, searching to have this vision reinforced by community or communities subordinates the external world to personal imagination.

CONCLUSION

This observation should not be taken as a criticism of these theories as much as an observation about the nature of identity formation. Returning to Hegel, it is possible to see the inevitable proclivity of every self-consciousness to see itself as the essential. William James posits that this is the case in "On a Certain Blindness in Human Beings." No matter how hard we try to recognize others, despite the good faith put forth in trying to imagine ourselves as a part of a community, we seem to look to community to reflect ourselves instead. "Now the blindness in human beings . . . is the blindness with which we all are afflicted in regard to the feelings of creatures and people different from ourselves" (James 1962, 259). Our imagination is limited. And in particular, limited when it comes to seeing others in the same terms as we see ourselves.

There are other reasons to be cautious of this version of identity confirmation through mutual recognition or community membership. First, the resolution of self and other through the development of a "we" wagers upon the desire for self-recognition to be forcefully, and equally, expressed by both parties. Yet power, will, or blindness can prevent mutuality from developing. Second, it is symptomatic of our culture's individualism that we would expect people to pursue individual identity above all else. In such an environment, when it comes to ourselves, when it comes to our own identities, our judgment can hardly be trusted. Third, as I will explore in more detail in Chapter 5, this emphasis upon having the world reflect one's identity privileges wealth. Recognition and redistributive politics are not as different as they initially appear. In a capitalist culture, wealth provides the foremost means to express and confirm one's identity. Identity, community, and consumption come to be linked together in an oftentimes inauspicious fashion.

Ultimately, then, the key to the relationship between identity and community is recognizing the limitations of imagination and self-consciousness rather than vainly seeking to overcome or compensate for them. It is interesting to consider Hegel's other solution to the master-slave dialectic. The slave interacts with the world and is forced to experience the limits of his imagination. The phenomenal world is unyielding, and often unaffected by the way we imagine ourselves to be. Perhaps materiality is more forceful in bringing us to a recognition of the boundaries of our desires and the establishment of the boundaries of the self. Paradoxically, recognizing the boundaries of the imagined self also empowers the imagination. The slave is rewarded with a new, true recognition of the bounds of human possibility and himself specifically. It may seem counterintuitive to consider taking the position of the slave. But the possibility that we might discover who we are through less than ideal circumstances seems worth entertaining. The interaction between imagination and the world is where the true potential to find oneself lies. And, as I argue elsewhere, this is also where the power to create liberatory politics also resides. The ultimate purpose of politics should be not only to empower the individual imagination, but also to change the world. Experiencing the limitations, obstacles, and restrictions upon worldly existence is a crucial element in formulating both self consciousness and political consciousness.

The vision of community as seamless marriage between self and other means that we might limit the experience of community to being an extension of self. Here imagination needs to be challenged rather than indulged. Our imaginations cannot and should not be sheltered from our world. This fact should not be taken as a death blow to oppositional thinking, but rather as the necessary condition of its realization.

3

HABITS OF THE HEARTH
Families and Politics in Theory and Practice

> Like every living being I am searching for an idea of the State, but what I find is the problem of the family.
>
> —LUCE IRIGARAY, *Sexes and Genealogies*

In "The Difficulty of Imagining Others" Elaine Scarry (1999) builds upon the supposition that we simply cannot imagine others in a way that provides for morality, equality, and respect. To rectify this problem, she suggests that we employ institutions to aid our failed imaginations. While she does not elaborate specifics, working from her basic observation I can offer some concrete examples of how institutions may help to create the effects of recognition, without having to rely solely upon the individual imagination. For example, what if the United States had an asylum law opening our borders to all refugees from areas where our military was deployed? Rather than relying upon our imagination to create empathy with those who suffer from our militarism, we would know that numerous refugees would come to live amongst us. This very clear, institutionally mandated consequence would certainly bolster our ability to imagine those in what too often seem to be distant or inconceivable locations.

In the previous chapter I argued that seeing imagination in relation to material circumstances helps to prevent both narcissistic projection and apolitical disconnection. Institutions are key elements of these circumstances, so in this and the following chapter, I look at attempts to create community via reform of political institutions. Proposals to reform current institutions to protect, create, or empower communities mirror Scarry's suggestion. Liberalism provokes these attempts to correct its impersonalism, thus naturally shaping the character of its opposition. Looking at how we conceptualize family, civil society, and the state in relationship to the possibilities of community demonstrates how the political landscape often directs political imagination. Nonetheless, political imagination can also remold this landscape.

THE PROBLEM OF THE FAMILY

The Hegelian vision of the end of history, when the state delivers harmony between particularity and universalism, haunts us today. Many ideals of community espouse this balance between universalism and particularity, though in different terms. As I discuss in more detail in Chapter 4, the state is not considered the institution that can deliver this resolution for many reasons. But the political potential of two other institutions, the family and civil society, has been closely considered in the past ten years. Community is envisioned as a space of commonality that nonetheless allows for particularity, and these two institutions have been identified as locations where this interplay between personal and collective occurs.

Liberalism accommodates universalism and particularism by dividing society into two spheres, the public and private. In private we would be recognized and nourished according to our distinct circumstances and needs. Ideally, to prevent discrimination based upon particular identities, we would be seen only as abstract citizens in public. There we have a universal, generalized, and hence equal identity. One uniting element of all theorists of community I discuss is their dissatisfaction with this particular arrangement.

This chapter's epigraph demonstrates one critique of the liberal ideal of politics. The family becomes "a problem" for the universal citizenship of the state because families are one realm where inequality persists. As the admittedly banal example of tax codes reveals via the designation of someone as a "head of household," the differentiation of the family bleeds into the universalism of the state. Those who are perceived as less than equal in private cannot check their identities at the invisible barrier between public and private to achieve equal citizenship. Further, by claiming that all particularities can be sequestered in the private realm, the public realm can with impunity ignore the particular needs of different populations. In theory, ignoring particularity in public is a way of achieving equality. Some feminist and critical race theorists point out that in practice, ignoring particularity is a way of perpetuating inequality. Removing the conceptual division between public and private is therefore seen as a way to achieve equality in both mutually interdependent spheres.

From another perspective, the division between public and private is problematic because it impoverishes the public realm. Noting the natural affection, mutuality, and commitment that are evident in families, some theorists claim that if we make public institutions resemble private ones, we can revitalize public life and make participation more satisfying and compelling. Thus, civic communitarians want to revitalize public life by removing the barrier between public and private life (Barber 1975; Elshtain 1981, 1982a, 1982b). Feminists who embrace an ethics of care also see the values of the family as a way to make the public more welcoming and just (Alpert 1973; Ruddick 1980; Gilligan 1982; Tronto 1993; Kittay 1999; Minow 1999).

Both perspectives look to institutions that are situated on the margins between public and private, the family and civil society, as potential locations to accomplish their different goals. Interestingly, these debates about family and civil society try to articulate a new vision of politics that is based on community and that creates institutions capable of promoting our ability to imagine others. Doing so would create increased empathy and commitment as a way to fundamentally change a political order that values competition and individualism. In this chapter I will focus on the arguments about the political importance of families and the values that they transmit in American democracy. In the following chapter, I examine how ideals of community have championed civil society, public participation, and the public sphere at the same time they have viewed the state with suspicion. The two chapters together offer an analysis of how ideals of community have been used to suggest institutional reform of American politics over the past ten years.

BEYOND PUBLIC AND PRIVATE

Delineating between public and private is a difficult task, and much ink has been spilled trying to articulate the proper relationship, or boundary, between public and private life. What is most important to keep in mind is that *neither public nor private sphere exists*. They are conceptual tools that help us to schematize what we intuitively know: environments are different from each other, and they require and encourage us to behave in different ways. Hence becoming a fully actualized person requires that we experience multiple contexts that help us to develop in ways particular to each of them.

Public and private is an overly simplified dichotomy that has little empirical foundation. After all, cannot one have an intimate private meeting in a state legislative building? Or a neighborhood meeting at one's house? Whether the sidewalk in front of your house is considered public property or private responsibility depends upon the state of your municipality's finances and its traditions. Courts cannot decide whether shopping malls are public or private places either. It often depends upon the socioeconomic class of the parties involved.

By asserting that public and private spheres do not exist, I do not mean to imply that the delineation of public and private does not matter. On the contrary, as the example of the shopping mall suggests, public and private are designations that are used to great effect. Feminist scholars in particular have explored how the delineation of public and private realms has been used to subordinate women. It is often mistakenly assumed that the division of public and private somehow trapped women in the home, relegating them to the private sphere. Instead, the impact of the division of public and private was to obscure the true nature of the home, as a location of reproduction *and* production, inequality, and sometimes abuse (MacKinnon 1989; Glenn 1992; Stacey 1990, 1996). The designation of public and private spheres in the United States is more accurately understood as the distinction between spheres of government regulation and those that exist largely outside of it. There are, of course, deviations from this formula but this is ultimately where the distinction rests. Regulation over private life and business, as profuse as it actually is, is still seen as an *exception*.

Hence debates about public and private distinctions can become a morass. The designation is not really an empirical one, no matter how hard we try to establish what makes a space public and what makes it private, yet it does have a tremendous impact on our lives. Furthermore, the difference between public and private does reflect the knowledge that social environments are distinct from one another—yet at the same time the designation often obscures the nature of this difference.

In addition to these problems, we must view the debates about public and private in the United States in their historical context. It is hard to say which image is more cherished—man's home as his castle or the public arena where he comes together with other citizens to form the backbone of the republic. Depending upon one's political proclivities, one can argue that either sphere is equally endangered. Technological surveillance and fear of terrorism threaten to smash whatever remnants of our so-called privacy continue, while public meetings and membership in voluntary organizations have fallen precipitously according to others. If the two spheres are drawn in relation to one another, one might in fact ask how it is that both seem to be growing smaller.

Ideals of community drive an interest in social life, in belonging to a larger group. The problem is that belonging to large groups does not always provide a very fulfilling type of membership. We want to imagine a public existence that is rewarding, one that acknowledges us for who we are, as articulated in the last chapter. The challenge, then, is to envision the kinds of institutions that would foster this recognition and self-actualization. It is clear that the debate about the appropriate demarcation of public and private is really about trying to build a world that seems most rewarding in both a communal and an intimate regard.

Aristotle began the tradition of mapping human activities and capacities into different spatial arenas in *The Politics* (1969). He understood the family as part of the household, a realm concerned with economic commerce and the provision of life's necessities. The household realm, for Aristotle, is further characterized by relationships that are "by nature" unequal. These associations are suited to the overall purpose of the household, which is the maintenance of life. The *polis*, or political realm, has a different purpose, namely, achieving the good life. Relations between citizens require a fundamental equality so that all participants can both rule and be ruled, and thereby keep the perspective of those being ruled in mind. Restricting access to the public realm for those who are "by nature" equals means that democratic participation can be realized as an ideal. The equality of one sphere contrasts to the inequality of the other.

One of the great accomplishments of early liberal theory was the inversion of this relationship: the private realm, understood as an enlarged sphere of commerce that happened both inside and outside of the household, was the realm of personal freedom. The state, considered the political or public realm, exists in order to adjudicate conflicts in the private realm (Locke 1988). State interference creates inequality in the private sphere, where, according to this view, it is assumed that all participants have equal opportunity. Therefore, equality bestowed "by nature" eradicates the need to establish equality through political means. But considering all nongovernmental activity as "private" disregards cooperative activity that may be outside of state control, but is nevertheless "public" in the sense that it involves acting in concert, establishing coalition, exercising power, engaging in debate about issues that have importance for a number of people, or some combination thereof. Consequently, the division between public and private spheres of activity is a slippery one. Is it the location of an activity that defines its status as public or private; is it the number of people that are involved; or does the state genuinely hold the monopoly on all "public" activities?[1]

DEMOCRACY AND FAMILY

> When the American returns from the turmoil of politics to the bosom of the family, he immediately finds a perfect picture of order and peace. There all his pleasures are simple and natural and his joys innocent and quiet, and as the regularity of life brings him happiness, he easily forms the habit of regulating his opinions as well as his tastes. (Alexis de Tocqueville 1969, 291)

The relationship between families and politics is a difficult one to articulate. Families were originally taken as the model for political life (paternalism), then deliberately segregated from it. Today, this separation and difference from public life is now taken as the source of the family's political import. Families are units where mutuality is emphasized. Do they serve as a point of resistance in an individualistic world? Or does the power configuration of the family complement that of other institutions?

Social contract theorists saw that it would be difficult to reconcile self-rule with paternalism: if the fathers could rule in one sphere, why could they not rule in another? The solution at the time was to divide society into public and private spheres. The private sphere, ideally governed by love, would be removed from impersonal contractual relationships that demanded self-legislation. The equality of the public sphere demanded both the restriction of inequality and the necessity for obedience to the private. Kant argued that "the public use of one's reason must always be free, and it alone can bring about enlightenment among mankind; the private use of reason may, however, often be narrowly restricted, without otherwise hindering the progress of enlightenment" (Kant 1983, 42). As has been well established, the inequalities of one sphere affect the other. But the difference between the two realms has been an integral part of American liberal democracy from its beginning—it is the complementarity of the spheres that pervades our cultural understanding of the family as a political institution.

Tocqueville was the first to comment on the unique relationship between family and politics in a democratic polity. The absence of paternalism and primogeniture made the bonds of the family less calculated and hence

---

1. See Wientraub and Kumar (1997) for several excellent essays about this problematic division.

governed more by "natural affection" (Tocqueville 1969, 584–89). The loss of formal public hierarchy and the promotion of individualism broke apart traditional social ties, thereby strengthening the importance of the family in providing the social mores and bonds necessary to human existence. "Democracy loosens social ties, but it tightens natural ones. At the same time as it separates citizens, it brings kindred closer together" (589). Tocqueville emphasizes that the family provides a crucial support to a democratic and individualistic polity, inculcating virtue, moderating self-interest, and preparing children for future independence. Precisely because the public realm has become less communally oriented, the family must be redefined to become more so. It is the individualism of one sphere that contrasts with the interdependence of the other.

That this arrangement was accomplished through a fiercely gendered division of activities did not trouble Tocqueville. The ideology of Republican Motherhood that predominated in the United States during the nineteenth century proposed that women performed a vital political function by staying at home to raise good citizens. In *Democracy in America,* Tocqueville observed that this was necessary since democracy allowed women more freedom within their realm than in aristocratic regimes and required that all children be brought up to use their democratic freedom responsibly. Tocqueville claimed that "Americans do not think that man and woman have the duty or the right to do the same things, but they show an equal regard for the part played by both and think of them as beings of equal worth, though their fates are different" (603). Accordingly, embracing domestic duties and social subordination is the path toward "moral superiority" on the part of American women. Segregation from politics and the marketplace enables women to uphold the highest ethical standards, which they then transmit to their children.

Following Tocqueville, theorists of natural and civic community assert the crucial importance of institutions that mediate between individuals and the state as "the seedbeds of virtue" necessary for the maintenance of a liberal democracy. Without these institutions, the liberal democratic order is threatened. Here, David Blankenhorn makes a statement of this position that is emblematic of communitarian literature on the topic. "The family is the cradle of the civil society; the essential foundation upon which the rest of civil society depends. Consequently, a weakening family system almost certainly signals a weakening civil society. In short, as the family goes, so (probably) goes the civil society" (Blankenhorn and Glendon 1995, 275). The family serves an integral function in the liberal political order by producing the next generation of good citizens. Ultimately, this means that "parents have a moral responsibility to the community to invest themselves in the proper upbringing of their children." Because the root of most social problems is children "who have not been brought up properly," parenting "is not merely a personal, private matter" (54, 68). Instead, the main purpose of the family is to ensure that future members of the "national community" will be good citizens.

Blankenhorn and others of this persuasion argue that a politics based upon impersonal, contractual relations has failed to sustain the moral order necessary in a democratic society. Because families embody "private virtues," they can provide an ethical model for politics. For example, Michael Sandel has suggested that the family illustrates a form of justice that is not impersonal. In *Liberalism and the Limits of Justice*, he argues that because we live in a political system that mediates between strangers, impersonal justice has developed as the ideal method of ensuring fairness. The liberal idea of justice assumes that "we cannot know each other well enough for love to serve alone" (Sandel 1982, 172). Sandel asserts that this procedural form of justice actually reinforces our isolation from one another because it presumes that we will always be strangers to one another. He argues, in support of John Rawls's view, against the idea that justice has to be understood as mediation between rights-bearing individuals in modern society (Rawls 1971). "Consider for example a more or less ideal family situation, where relations are governed in large part by spontaneous affection and where, in consequence, the circumstances of justice prevail to a relatively small degree. Individual rights and fair decision procedures are seldom invoked, not because injustice is rampant but because their appeal is pre-empted by a spirit of generosity in which I am rarely inclined to claim my fair share" (Sandel 1982, 33). The family provides the model for association that does not need to invoke the principle of justice because those involved have a clear perception of common good.

Similarly, some feminist scholars have argued that revaluing what have been viewed as "women's activities" and "women's morality" can both better serve women and potentially revolutionize politics. For example, in "The Concrete and Generalized Other," Seyla Benhabib argues that if we can see "the other" with specific characteristics, that person's universal rights will be safer. The morality of "the generalized other" that Benhabib characterizes as "respect, duty, worthiness and dignity" will be awarded only when complemented by the morality of the "concrete other," whose specificity generates "love, care and sympathy and solidarity" (Benhabib 1992,

159). Martha Minow (1999), Joan Tronto (1993), Eva Feder Kittay (1999), and Nancy Hirschmann (1992) have all embarked on the project of rescuing moral solidarity, obligation, and care-giving, endowing them with an equal—if not superior—status to the rules of autonomy that predominate society.

As even this cursory and incomplete list suggests, the problem is gendered. Making public what has been assumed to be private virtue has long held ideological appeal in American politics. First-wave feminists, prohibitionists, and abolitionists all used the argument before recent communitarian campaigns on behalf of families and faith-based initiatives (Cott 1987). But the assumption that the public/private divide works to retain virtue is problematic. First, the division of life into public and private spheres was never complete, nor was the relegation of women to home ever fully accomplished. The division of labor was not so strict in African American families, nor in the families of the working class. The accolades of Republican Motherhood were only available for women attached to men of secure financial standing (Ryan 1990, 1997; Glenn 1992; Coontz 1992). Second, although it may be true that many men viewed women as virtuous within the private realm, it does not follow that women were thereby considered to be voices of morality in the public realm. For example, Mary Ryan provides an excellent example of how quickly private virtue is defiled when made public. She reprints an Army poster from 1862 declaring that any woman expressing her contempt for Union soldiers would be "treated as a woman of the town plying her vocation" (Ryan 1990, 2–3). Similarly, "public woman," "woman of the town," and "street walker" are all synonyms for prostitutes (Wilson 1991). Finally, and most important, saving the virtue of women by relegating them to the private sphere was a most effective way to separate women from all institutions (commerce, politics, education) that could provide them some power or independence. The virtuousness of the private realm was a poor prize in comparison to the corrupt power available in more public pursuits (Pateman 1989; Eisenstein 1981).

The gendered nature of the division between public and private demands attention to the power differentials involved in the split. Both feminist reevaluations of ethics and the communitarian support for the besieged family attempt to create an inversion of this power dynamic. But it is the complementary inegalitarianism of the two spheres that gives them their characters. Give women more power, or truly privilege the family in politics—for example by instituting a minimum wage that supports families, providing free, high-quality day care, or putting in place thirty-hour work week for all people—and the nature of the family would fundamentally change. Reflecting on Tocqueville's observations, it seems clear that the institution of the family is an integral element in maintaining institutions of liberal democracy. Rather than assuming that the family as it exists is a repository of natural affect, Tocqueville's description places the family in historical and political context. In fact, our propensity to view the family as "natural" as opposed to "social" reflects the widespread acceptance of social contract theory, rather than making any statement about the "true" nature of families. The family is "natural" only because we prefer to see its existence as a priori and unregulated. So the question is whether or not we can reform, or even overturn, liberal individualism with one of the institutions that it created.

FAMILIES, CITIZENSHIP, AND INDIVIDUALISM

Another way of looking at the issue is to ask whether familial authority can transform children into good citizens. Susan Moller Okin (1979, 1989) has argued that the inequities of power in families actually make them rather poor training grounds for democratic citizenship. Okin observes that "the hierarchical nature of the family made it an exemplary socializing agent for the hierarchical world of king and subjects" (Okin 1979, 287). Until the family itself is democratized, it cannot serve the function of inculcating children into democratic citizenship. She suggests that familial justice and public justice are antithetical:

> It may seem uncontroversial, even obvious, that families must be just because of the vast influence that they have on the moral development of children. But this is clearly not the case ... unless the first and formative example of adult interaction usually experienced by children is one of justice and reciprocity, rather than of domination and manipulation or of unequal altruism and one-sided sacrifice, and unless they themselves are treated with concern and respect, they are likely to be considerably hindered in becoming people who are guided by principles of justice. (17)

One might well also ask, if families teach children the virtues of sharing, communal responsibility, and obligation, how is it that these children are good citizens in a country that values independence and individualism?

Jessica Benjamin's work on domination, *The Bonds of Love: Psychoanalysis, Feminism, and the Problem of Domination,* provides an excellent summation of how it is that the domestic sphere turns men into able individuals in public. The entire process depends upon the gendered division of economic and social spheres, which dictates that women stay at home and provide care, voluntary work, and nurturance, while men go out into the world and maintain economic position, political opinion, and social prestige. The division of activities balances out all of the necessities of life, as long as both men and women are willing to combine in a partnership. Benjamin notes,

> The unbreachable line between public and private values rests on the tacit assumption that women will continue to preserve and protect personal life, the task to which they have been assigned. In this way the political morality can sustain the fiction of the wholly independent individual, whose main concern is a system of rights that protects him from other individuals like himself. The public world is conceived as a place in which direct recognition and care for others' needs is impossible—and this tolerable as long as the private world "cooperates." (Benjamin 1988, 197)

Caring for others, empathy, and cooperation are segregated into the home, making it possible to maintain a public sphere of all against all. The home provides a respite from the values of individualism, and in so doing makes it possible for the public sphere to remain atomized. However, this balance of public and private does not accord with the idea in American culture that citizens are supposed to be self-made men, dependent upon no other. So the question is, how exactly is the interdependence of the private sphere acceptable? Benjamin points out that women have not been, and still are not, seen as individual subjects in the same way that men are; therefore dependence upon them is safe.

The maternal bosom provides a haven for everyone. There is no need to remain strong there, precisely because the mother figure does not have enough power to threaten others in the outside world. Benjamin writes:

> I believe that this insistence on the division between public and private is sustained by the fear that anything public or "outside" would merely intensify individual helplessness, that only the person we have not recognized as outside (mother and wife) can be

trusted to provide us with care, that the only safe dependence is on someone who is not part of the struggle of all against all, and indeed, who is herself not independent. Thus we can only protect our autonomy and mask our vulnerability by keeping nurturance confined to its own sphere. (202)

In other words, it is safe to be emotionally dependent upon women because they remain socially and economically dependent upon men. The safe dependence of the private sphere makes public autonomy tenable.

For one example of how idealizations of the importance of the private realm actually work to protect state, military, and economic interests, consider a recent decision by the United States Supreme Court. In the summer of 2001, the court upheld a regulation in Nguyen v. INS that distinguishes between children of American women and children of American men who are born abroad. If an American male fathers a child who is born outside the country, the child is not granted citizenship automatically; instead the father must legally acknowledge the child and apply for his or her citizenship. In contrast, if an American woman has a child abroad with a citizen of another country, the child is automatically granted citizenship if the mother has lived in the United States for at least one consecutive year of her life. The reason stated for this differentiation? The mother's presence at her child's birth provides a unique opportunity or potential to develop relationships that support citizenship, while biology provides no such natural bonds between fathers and their offspring. The valorization of motherhood is also its denigration.

As I have demonstrated, the invocation of mother right as the source of true citizenship is a long tradition in American thought. This court decision denies any sort of national responsibility for, or even linkage to, the thousands of children who are fathered by American soldiers stationed abroad. As Cynthia Enloe has established, the military has a vested interest in allowing and even encouraging soldiers to have sex with local women, whether through prostitution, romantic liaisons, or, in some cases, rape (Enloe 2000). The links between virility, masculinism, and militarism mean that sexual advances usually accompany any military deployment. The idealization of the links between motherhood and citizenship protects American soldiers, and their country, from the consequences of their actions.

Families were originally units of both production and reproduction. Mary Ryan has studied the links between the development of industrial production and the idealization of womanhood in antebellum America (1979,

1981). As production assumed a larger scale, "opportunities for advancement were open only to those with the right to hold, control, and alienate property—that is, adult men" (Ryan 1979, 162). Alice Kessler-Harris's work demonstrates that the "family wage" developed at this same historical juncture, making it possible for some men to support some women in idleness, or rather, in consumption (Kessler-Harris 1990). While romantic marriage became a precious ideal, women's economic dependence was actually deepened, causing one contemporary observer to call marriage "the hardest way on earth of getting a living" (Ryan 1979, 163).

Defining the family as a private sphere that engaged only in reproduction made the work still accomplished in the home invisible. Poor women (usually nonwhite women or immigrants) worked in the homes of wealthy women, as they do today in increasing numbers (Glenn 1992; Ehrenreich 2001). Many women worked at home, producing food or bringing in piece work. Remarkably, once again manufacturers are finding that having women work in their own homes is a way of avoiding many costs, as well as labor regulations. Domestic workers have become an international export strategy, enabling countries to meet their debt repayments, yet the home is still regarded as the "domestic sphere" (Constable 1997; Chang 2000). The divide of public and private continues to hide the mobilization of the domestic sphere by the market. Dividing society into different spheres is a proven strategy for maintaining inequality alongside the rhetoric of equality. It has taken a great deal of effort to lift the veil obscuring the nuclear family in order to procure its regulation, for example, in cases of domestic violence.

In conclusion, these theorists who see the family as embattled have seized upon a genuine problem in market relations and the mechanics of the bureaucratic state. These institutions are dehumanizing and alienating. Political life can be more compelling, and we need a new vision of political participation as something more than voting. Furthermore, the role of families in maintaining institutions of liberal democracy has been undervalued for too long. But seeing how bourgeois nuclear families play an integral role in maintaining liberal capitalism creates an ambiguous political agenda. Do we want to resurrect the family wage, making it possible for a male to support an entire family, as in the past? Do we want all women and men to do the things that only privileged women did in the past?

What is striking is that these debates tend to misdiagnose the source of the family's very real illness. Families do not suffer from an excess of individualism (at least not more today than in the past), nor are they suffering from feminism or a morality of autonomy. Rather, fewer families in the United States provide a respite from the world's challenges because the demands of global capitalism have become ever greater. The family wage is a distant memory, and even two-income households increasingly struggle to maintain a decent standard of living. If families don't eat dinner together anymore, it is not because no one values families, but rather because too frequently parents are working.

To blame the crisis in family life on families is to engage in victim bashing. Championing the family above other values will only valorize families with enough wealth to provide the luxury of flexible scheduling and quality time, and stigmatize those who do not share this opportunity. The material circumstances of working families must change to provide a real revolution of the political landscape. The collision course between the reproductive and productive needs of society is most evident in the once again raging debates in some circles about whether women should work.[2] The question is not how to value choices and the women and men who make them, but to ask how such choices could be made available to all families.

Although I do believe that this debate misdiagnoses the problem with "the American family," I do think that it offers a number of important contributions to my larger argument. First, to speak of "the family" as an institution, as many of the feminist and communitarian theories do, reveals that these debates pivot upon the issue of the political imagination. After all, there is no *one family*, and no family could embody everything "the family" is supposed to be. Nor does the institution of the family even try to acknowledge the multiplicity of family arrangements that actually exists. Debates about the family are normative rather than descriptive. They are about imagining the ways we want families to be, or think they ought to be.

Michael Ignatieff observed, "Whenever I try to imagine a future other than the one towards which we seem to be hurtling, I find myself dreaming a dream of the past" (Ignatieff 1984, 107). Our institutions are traces of the world as it was once imagined. Ideals about families changed with industrialization. This is not to say that all families became this vision but, rather, that all families were measured against it. We have created laws, tax codes, government regulations, labor practices, child-rearing philosophies,

---

2. In November 2003, the *New York Times Magazine* ran a cover article about working mothers that generated a historical volume of mail. In the following months, other journals and countless talk shows resurrected the topic. One encouraging aspect of these debates is that not all of them blame the working mother for children's problems or view the stay at home mother as a saint. Instead, the nature of work requirements is coming under increasing scrutiny. However, during the same time a woman in Connecticut was blamed for her son's suicide because she was a bad housekeeper. This fact was offered as proof that she failed to provide a proper home.

normative psychology, and occupational divisions based upon this ideal of families. Some of these practices seem to be increasingly difficult to uphold. Will this in turn lead to a rejection of the way the family was imagined? Thus far, it seems only to have strengthened our nostalgia for the imaginary family of the past as a respite from the pressures of institutions and practices that were created as a complement to "the family."

Institutions are trajectories of imagination that persist, shaping the way we imagine in times to come. The way we imagine the family is heavily dependent upon institutions of liberal capitalism. Therefore, revalorizing the family, *as it is currently imagined*, is not an effective way to offer an alternative to liberal capitalism.

The lesson I offer from this discussion is that institutions and their logics provide a thick lens that influences the way we imagine political possibilities. This is not new to political scientists who study the importance of political institutions. I suggest that we examine the attempts to change institutions with a few caveats in mind. It would be wise to consider the origin and original function of the institution in question. Remembering the historical context of institutions is crucial for correctly evaluating how they function. Also, how an institution is imagined to function must be distinguished from how it actually does function. Most critically, it is necessary to consider whether the means of transforming the institution are themselves a result of the very conditions that created it in the first place. Attempts at reform will fail if they lack a new way of imagining the relationship between the world and the institution.

My concern in this and the next chapter is that the way we imagine alternatives to liberal, individualist capitalism are too embedded in liberal, individualist capitalism. When we look to the family to save us from the state of the world, we engage in a nostalgia for an imagined past that does not serve to create an alternative future. Creating a world that is more communal entails imagining different kinds of communities, not looking at the small spaces where they are idealized within the current political and social system.

4

CITIZENS WITHOUT STATES?
Bringing Community into Institutions

The state has always been viewed with a certain amount of distrust in the United States. Even with its tentacles firmly bound by separation of powers, popular election, federalism, and bureaucratic process, it is a commonplace belief that the state is an interfering evil only slightly less dangerous than the alternative—anarchy. Public opinion polls routinely demonstrate that Americans distrust their government, even as they regard it as an ineffective, distant mechanism grinding away taxpayer money.

The state is equally out of favor in contemporary political theory. One could trace this aversion to the minimalist approach to governance advocated by classical liberal theorists. But communitarian and feminist alternatives to liberalism provide no exception to this minimalist trend. This is curious because one of the primary objections to liberalism is that it is an essentially apolitical understanding of social organization.[1] It is perhaps this reluctance to consider the state as an instrument of social change and political possibilities that reveals how completely these alternative theories remain in the shadow of the liberal world view.

In part, the inspiration to write about the state came from the success of the Parité movement in France, where feminists fruitfully lobbied for a constitutional amendment requiring all parties to present a slate of candidates equal in number of men and women. Parties whose candidates are not fifty percent women will be denied state electoral funds, generally the sole source of campaign financing in France. A similar strategy would be impossible in the United States given the structure of our political parties and our highest bidder campaign financing. Yet aside from these institutional

---

1. Hannah Arendt (1958, 1963) and Sheldon Wolin (1960) provided early versions of this argument. See also Michael Sandel (1996a); Benjamin Barber (1984); Jean Bethke Elshtain (1995); Chantal Mouffe (1993); Zillah Eisenstein (1981); Carol Pateman (1970); Seyla Benhabib (1996); and Anne Phillips (1993).

differences, I was most struck by the interest in using the state as an instrument of feminist politics. Les Paritaires are inherently neither conservative nor naive. They do not see the state as anything but a tainted instrument, an integral element in patriarchal, bourgeois rule.[2] They espouse complex views about the dangers of universalism and see representation as anything but transparent. In virtually every regard, these women would find themselves in an easy dialogue with anti-institutional leftists in the United States.

Why, then, expend precious energy to put women in office? The only answer to this question seems to be historical—I suspect Les Paritaires may have garnered some inspiration from the Communards whose names are memorialized on the Paris streets they walk. In 1891 Engels noted that the transformation of the state from the servant of society into its master was most complete in the United States (Marx and Engels 1966, 16). The Paris Commune of 1871 was the most concerted attempt to reverse this tendency in France. Engels writes that by creating universal suffrage and popular recall of officials, by renouncing the pecuniary advantages of office, and by using government power to dismantle class privilege, "The communal Constitution would have restored to the social body all the forces hitherto absorbed by the state parasite feeding upon, and clogging the free movement of society" (70–71). The Communards may have met a brutal end in Père Lachaise, but clearly their ability to imagine that the state can be used for entirely different purposes than it always has been remains alive.

I bring up Parité and the Paris Commune to serve as a point of contrast to the status of politics in the United States, which is my main concern. How do ideals of community confront the power of the state? In this chapter, I demonstrate how ideals of belonging, participation, and civil society combine with liberal biases against the state to create a particularly strange political configuration: a valorization of citizenship alongside a rejection of government.

In contrast to the antipathy shown to the state, political theorists and political scientists generally embrace the idea of civil society. Theorists are inspired by Habermas's description of a bourgeois public sphere that served as a bulwark against market forces and the nation-state apparatus (Habermas 1989). More recently, civil society was hailed as the David that slew the Communist Goliath in the former Soviet bloc, and political scientists have begun a rediscovery of the connections between civil society and democracy.

Habermas and other recent theorists see the relationship between the

---

2. Two excellent sources on the Parité movement in France that are available in English are a special issue on Parité of *differences* (1997, 9:2) and Kramer (2000).

state and civil society as antagonistic. The state is an ungracious presence in participatory politics, setting the agenda, creating and enforcing rules to serve particular constituencies, and often silencing, rather than mediating, dissenting viewpoints. Similarly, as the decline of Soviet power suggests, an active civil society can effectively challenge state power. Theories of community inform debates about civil society and the state, helping to point out what is missing from the state and proposing civil society as the alternative. Communities are considered optimal locations for encouraging and sustaining participation of their members. Via the lens of participation, the state is clearly lacking and civil society holds great promise. In this chapter, I want to examine debates about the state, participation, community, and civil society. To do so in an exhaustive sense would be impossible. What I do want to accomplish is to demonstrate ways that ideals of community have been critically applied to American liberal democracy and to suggest an alternative way of relating community and the state.

ON CIVIL SOCIETY

Looking at cultural institutions and practices is a welcome proposition in the study of politics. Yet it is important to remember that the concept of civil society contains many ambiguities that are often not acknowledged in the blush of our reacquaintance with the notion. It is not at all clear to me what civil society is, who it is, what it encompasses, and why it seems automatically to create democracy. Do bowling clubs really count as civil society? Is it the act of speaking to others that bolsters democracy? Is it where we learn to listen to one another? With these reservations expressed, I wish to reiterate that for many political thinkers, civil society is a sort of heavenly sphere, where all of the world's inequalities are segregated from its boundaries (Putnam 1993, 1995; Lipset 1996; Fukuyama 1995).

One reason civil society is particularly attractive as a concept is that it allows theorists to overcome the troubling public/private divide discussed in the preceding chapter. Yet it does not provide a clear solution to the ambiguities of this divide. In fact, understandings of civil society are, if anything, even more disparate than conceptualizations of public and private realms. Just to begin, some thinkers, such as Habermas, consider civil society as part of a public sphere. Others propose that it is neither public nor private. Thinkers such as Jean Cohen and Andrew Arato (1992) see economics as distinct from civil society, revising Hegel's original formulation. Civil society may be a collection of smaller groups, as the work of Tocqueville suggests. Or it may be considered a singular entity in the sense that it is a location where a particular kind of activity occurs. Civil society is sometimes considered neither public nor private; at other times, it has spheres that are both public and private.

Communitarians such as Benjamin Barber and Jean Bethke Elshtain have started referring to themselves as "civil society communitarians."[3] They argue that in the United States, political arguments have been centered either on the individual (as in laissez-faire liberal capitalism) or on state regulation (as in democratic socialism). Communitarians on both left and right argue that the liberal conception of politics privileges the individual and the bureaucratic state, taking politics away from its proper location—the community. They see civil society as a social forum that is not controlled by the state and think that it is the location of community-based politics.

Political theorists have seized on the notion of civil society as a potential corrective to the bureaucratized relationships and activities that characterize economics and government. Michael Walzer has defined civil society as "the space of uncoerced human association and also the set of relational networks—formed for the sake of family, faith, interest, and ideology—that fill this space" (Walzer 1995, 7). Although Walzer defines civil society spatially, it is clear that all of the activities to which he alludes could not be conducted in a space that could be delineated. Family picnics, corporate board meetings, and confessions to a priest all happen in different settings, and necessarily so. Instead, the key to Walzer's definition is his use of the word "uncoerced." Rather than actually being a space, he proposes that civil society is a kind of phenomenology—a place where everyone can "be themselves" and have relationships that are somehow untainted by power.

This definition of civil society as the space of "genuine relations" pervades communitarian literature. Different communitarians use different methods of formulating this idea. For example, Robert Bellah adopts Habermas's notion of "system" and "lifeworld" and laments the invasion of the "lifeworld" by the market. The state can do a part in controlling the market, but "strengthening not only the family but the larger 'lifeworld'—what is often called civil society—is critical" (Bellah 1990, 235). *The Responsive Community* published an editorial by former Senator Bill Bradley (1995) that echoes Bellah's juxtaposition of a virtuous civil society with the tainted relations of the state and market.

---

3. Both thinkers used this term in September 1998 at the American Political Science Convention to describe their political persuasion. In my introduction I refer to this position as Civic Community.

This idea of civil society as the location of genuine relationships is the basis of the communitarian proposal for a different kind of politics. For example, David Blankenhorn suggests "the civil society strategy" as the core of a "third way" of politics, neither laissez-faire nor socialist (Blankenhorn, Bayme, and Elshtain 1990). In this view, civil society is the location of communitarian politics, but it does not function as an intermediary realm between individuals and the state. This version of civil society is not an intersection of individual and universal interests, but rather a bulwark *against* them.

Feminists interested in movement politics, however, have not been as taken by the idea of civil society. Jodi Dean offers an excellent summary of how feminists have approached civil society in *The Solidarity of Strangers* (Dean 1996, chap. 3). As she points out, there has been a surprising lack of interest in the idea, given that civil society seems ideally situated to overcome the division of public and private spheres. Indeed, the understanding of civil society as a space that is *both* public and private signals that feminist appropriations of the concept aim toward resisting rather than bolstering the status quo. Dean herself is enthusiastic about the revolutionary possibilities of civil society: "These spaces and possibilities for a democratic politics of difference and solidarity can be found in a revitalized civil society, a civil society conceived not in terms of an opposition between public and private spheres but as a variety of interconnecting discursive spheres" (75). Dean demonstrates how the critique of the public/private divide has often resulted in the ossification of these respective spheres—the private sphere is simplistically labeled as feminine, and the public sphere and the democratic possibilities therein are dismissed as masculinist. Civil society, characterized by communicative rationality and forms of recognition and solidarity that transcend universal/particularist identities, offers a location for inclusive, democratic politics.

While I wholeheartedly agree with Dean's assessment of the problems of feminist retrenchment of public and private, I pause when considering her solution. Several feminists have already registered concerns with the concepts of "public sphere" and "civil society" which are often used and understood interchangeably.[4] Mary Ryan (1992), Nancy Fraser (1992), and Joan Landes (1998), among other feminists, have criticized the idea of a single

---

4. I'm not entirely convinced that the two terms are the same. They certainly have different genealogies, and different spokespeople. Functionally, they seem to encompass a similar range of activities, and indicate sociality that is not state-generated. For that reason, my discussion will follow the merger of the two terms.

public sphere as inaccurate and dangerously homogenizing. Habermas has conceded the exclusive nature of the historical bourgeois public sphere of his early description, and agrees that today it is more appropriate to speak of multiple public spheres (1992). To assert that there always have been, and should be, multiple public spheres seems entirely necessary. On the other hand, if we can prove that there have always been these multiple public spheres, as the work of Mary Ryan does (1990, 1992, 1997), then how can we argue that they are the key to political emancipation if they have clearly failed to provide it so far?

Furthermore, the kinds of memberships and activities that do seem unquestionably part of civil society—for example, churches, environmental organizations, identity politics groups, and neighborhood associations—are totally diverse and do in fact promote different kinds of memberships. Some of these organizations promote public involvement, such as the PTA, while others actively discourage it, such as fundamentalist churches. Membership in a gay rights organization encourages an entirely different kind of identity, solidarity, and membership than belonging to a model train club. Can we really put these disparate groups into one category and claim that they serve the same function?

The concept of civil society is so ethereal that it lends itself to idealization. Of course all concepts are difficult to translate into the material world, but civil society seems a particularly difficult one to pin down. This leads to its idealization for various purposes and by different groups. Communitarians see civil society as a place without conflict, a place to have politics be intimate and more rewarding. To me this sounds impossible at best. At worst, it suggests coercion and programmatic co-optation. Yet is the feminist claim that civil society can be our own heavenly sphere of difference and inclusion, open discursive practice, and the practice of multiple identities any more realistic?

Finally, I am troubled by the tendency to assume that civil society and the market are separate entities. It is clear why those who are interested in the progressive potential of civil society would want to exile the corporation from its midst. Corporate life is participatory, but it is difficult to maintain that such participation is emancipatory. Furthermore, in practice, it seems that civil society and economic development have become linked. For example, civil society has become a catchword in developmental economics and postcommunist political rhetoric. Nongovernmental organizations and the United States government have all become extremely interested in bolstering "civil society" in countries around the world. This commitment is not merely rhetorical—it includes millions of dollars to build civil society in places like Bangladesh, Estonia, and Ethiopia. Sometimes this means helping to restore a bath house; at other times it seems to mean helping to fund a radio broadcast. Frequently it means supplying computers and technological infrastructure, such as phone lines. All of this can be seen in the spirit of creating communication and informal networks. It can also be seen as developing the bourgeoisie or late capitalist forms of social mediation. Civil society and capitalism are intricately connected in practice, if not in theory (Ehrenberg 1999, chap. 8). In fact, civil society as a reservoir of charity, sociability and citizenship has replaced the institution that used to serve these functions: the family.

As the theories of more conservative communitarians demonstrate, many are still reluctant to relinquish the steadfast belief that all homes are small utopias. The growth of industrial capitalism demanded the valorization of the nuclear family. Is it possible that there is a parallel dynamic in the recent romance with civil society? After all, the story is that civil society "defeated communism" and is making the world safe for democracy. What I suspect is that the concept of civil society is fostered to mitigate the inequalities inherent in emerging labor markets. Closer to home, civil society is pinpointed as the savior of our democratic way of life as actual participation in self-government plummets, the entire voting process is thrown into question, and wage inequalities increase to levels not seen for more than one hundred years. Civil society as it is currently defined, as a space that is neither public nor private, cannot address any of these pressing problems. Rather, "civil society" is a sphere that complements these abuses of state and economic power.

While I agree with the observation that increased participation is necessary and preferable, I do not see how civil society can substitute for a full-fledged reform of both market and state. Accordingly, I will now turn to recent ideas about the state and how they relate to community and participatory politics.

WHITHER THE STATE?

Communitarians and antiliberal feminists attempt to combine acknowledgment of each person's individual characteristics with the ideal of equality. Remarkably, the Hegelian formulation of politics has escaped endorsement by those searching for a resolution between universal and particular. After all, the Hegelian state is the transcendent body of its citizenry—all persons can realize their own manifestations of world spirit through the state. Hegelian civil society remains the sphere of particularities. The coexistence of each sphere provides for the reconciliation and presence of our particular selves as well as a space of universality, an embodied "we" (Hegel 1967).

The state, however, plays no such role in recent attempts to balance universal and particular. Instead, both antiliberal feminist and communitarian theories of the state and democracy can best be understood in reference to Karl Marx's distinction between human and political emancipation elaborated in "On the Jewish Question." In this work, Marx asserted that the state, by existing as a separate sphere, can banish particular prejudices, problems, and inequalities from its consideration. It was Marx's corrective to Hegel to observe that doing so provides for emancipation only in the sphere of governance. Formal political equality does not end social inequality. This is not to say that political emancipation is not a worthwhile goal. "Political emancipation certainly represents great progress. It is not, indeed, the final form of human emancipation *within* the framework of the prevailing social order" (Marx 1963, 15). The prevailing social order was, and remains, founded upon a division between state and civil society. The state awards rights and privileges based upon our universal citizenship; civil society is the location of who we are as distinct individuals. Marx describes this division as follows: "Finally, man as a member of civil society is identified with *authentic man, man* as distinct from citizen, because he is man in his sensuous, individual and *immediate* existence, whereas *political* man is only abstract, artificial man, man as an *allegorical, moral* person" (30). Therefore, political liberation is necessarily an abstraction from our sensuous and immediate existence. It depends upon a separation from our selves in favor of a disembodied, allegorical citizen. Political liberation occurs in a limited sphere, as feminists who were disappointed by the results of enfranchisement were able to surmise rather quickly. On the other hand, human emancipation occurs through dissolution of these two spheres—a melding of universal citizen and particular self becomes possible. "Human emancipation will only be complete when the real, individual man has absorbed into himself the abstract citizen; when as an individual man, in his everyday life, in his work, and in his relationships, he has become a *species-being;* and when he has recognized and organized his own powers as *social* powers so that he no longer separates this social power from himself as *political* power" (31).

The state is associated with a more limited form of emancipation, capable of delivering freedom to an abstracted self. As Marx so brilliantly articulates in this essay, because political emancipation is predicated upon the division of universal and particular, or state and civil society, such political goals need not be one's highest aspiration. Instead, one may envision an alternative regime, one in which we may be represented in our sensuous totality.

COMMUNITARIAN CRITIQUES OF THE STATE

Communitarian critiques of the state fall into one of three categories: the state reinforces a damaging individualism; it is simply irrelevant; or it is coercive, monopolizing political power and disempowering its citizens. I will present these arguments separately and have chosen three representative authors who advance each of these views: Mary Ann Glendon, Michael Sandel, and Benjamin Barber.

Mary Ann Glendon's book *Rights Talk: The Impoverishment of Political Discourse* (1991) is the most sustained and detailed communitarian argument about how the state reinforces individualism and prevents the growth of community in the United States. One helpful way of understanding Glendon's argument is to consider it as basically cultural. "Rights talk" is the language of our society, which undermines our ability to maintain the institutions of state and civil society. The vocabulary of rights is based upon individual assertion rather than common purpose or even rational argumentation.

> The most distinctive features of our American rights dialect are the very ones that are most conspicuously in tension with what we require in order to give a reasonably full and coherent account of what kind of society we are and what kind of polity we are trying to create; its penchant for absolute extravagant formulations, its near aphasia concerning responsibility, its excessive homage to individual independence and self-sufficiency, its habitual concentration on the individual and the state at the expense of the intermediate groups of civil society, and its unapologetic insularity. Not only does each of these traits make it difficult to give voice to common sense or moral institutions, they also impede development of the sort of rational political discourse that is appropriate

to the needs of a mature, complex, liberal, pluralistic republic. (Glendon 1991, 14)

Glendon's main objection, then, to "rights talk" is that it reinforces individualism by looking at citizens as singular rights-bearers; it precludes rational debate because rights "trump" all other considerations (It is my right to do so, therefore I will!); it defines politics according to either the state that delivers rights or the individuals that carry them, thereby discounting the importance of civil society; and, finally, it preempts any discussion of what is right, moral, or just through an excessive reliance upon already formulated principles.

Although Glendon argues that "rights talk" impedes the development of a mature republic, the state itself plays a key role in its own disfiguration. In addition to detailing the effects of "rights talk" on society, she also provides a comprehensive investigation of the state's role in perpetuating, and even advancing, this discourse. The courts repeatedly use the principle of individual rights as the final arbiter in conflicts of interest and values. Even more damaging is the particular interpretation of rights that has developed in our legal system. For instance, Glendon quotes Samuel Warren and Louis D. Brandeis from "The Right to Privacy": "That the individual shall have full protection in person and in property is a principle as old as the common law; but it has been found necessary from time to time to define anew the exact nature and extent of such protection. . . . Gradually the scope of these legal rights [to life, liberty, and property] broadened; and now the right to life has come to mean the right to enjoy life,—the right to be left alone" (47). Thus, although an emphasis upon rights implicitly favors an individualist conception of society, the act of defining these rights has also explicitly promoted a more alienated existence by protecting "the right to be left alone." Glendon is quick to point out that the United States Supreme Court did not invent this tradition, no matter how enthusiastically it follows it. Instead, "the notion was already implicit in the stories and images that migrated from the works of Hobbes, Locke, and Blackstone into American legal and popular culture" (48).

Glendon runs into a problem of causality here. She points out the liberal philosophical tenets that influenced the creation of the Bill of Rights in the first place, and that continue to exercise influence over crucial Supreme Court decisions. Her comparative examples are intended to demonstrate that the German and French states, influenced by different philosophical traditions, endorse a more communal version of both rights and responsibilities than their Anglo-American counterparts. Her contrast is instructive, and demonstrates alternative ways of conceiving the relationship of state, society, and citizen. But her historical analysis of the origins of our legal culture also has the effect of making laws seem like destiny. If our laws are a product of our history and culture, how can we change them without also changing our culture? Why change laws rather than changing the culture?

Ultimately, Glendon relies heavily on the idea of civil society and proposes that a revitalization therein may correct much that is amiss in the United States today. Glendon herself does not expect the state to serve as an instrument of social change, although some of her proposals for how the state can help to foster community are unique. She sees civil society as the location of real reform. Her attitude toward the relative importance of state and civil society is best summarized by the passage she quotes from Judge Learned Hand (whose endowed chair Glendon currently holds at Harvard University): "I often wonder whether we do not rest our hopes too much on constitutions, upon laws and upon courts. These are false hopes; believe me, these are false hopes. Liberty lies in the hearts of men and women; when it dies there, no constitution, no law, no court can save it; no constitution, no law, no court can even do much to help it. While it lies there it needs no constitution, no law, no court to save it" (143). This passage emphasizes the participatory aspect of civil society that Glendon finds essential. Civil society is where liberty is exercised and maintained; the state is an obstacle to surmount in order to get there.

Some communitarian theorists make the implicit statement that the state is irrelevant to their political reform by omitting it from their discussions.[5] However, in an essay titled "America's Search for a New Public Philosophy" (1996a) Michael Sandel makes the explicit argument that the era of the nation-state has come to an end. For the most part, the article is excerpted from *Democracy's Discontent: America in Search of a Public Philosophy* (1996b), detailing the collusion between monied interests and the development of what Sandel terms "the Procedural Republic." *Democracy's Discontent* is Sandel's meticulous reconstruction of an alternative, republican political philosophy in the United States. He argues that only in the twentieth century did capitalist interests succeed in instituting a largely bureaucratic state that discouraged public participation and any sort of normative deliberation. The book calls for a resurrection of this alternative

---

5. The communitarian platform articulated in Etzioni (1993, 1996a) tries to avoid state involvement. See also Selznick (1992); Barber (1984, 1998); Sandel (1982); Bellah (1985); and Taylor (1989) for examples of the absence of the state in communitarian political thought.

political orientation, stating that our continued prosperity and stability require a more engaged citizenry. Using past thinkers to define the American republican tradition has two effects in *Democracy's Discontent*. First, Sandel's plan to revitalize public life seems more a project in reconstruction than the radical call for participatory politics frequently heard among the left. Second, his invocation of community as the location of politics is distinctly tinged with nostalgia for Jefferson's agrarian farmer citizen and a way of life that is unmistakably gone in the United States.

Sandel's essay avoids this dynamic, however, by proposing an alternative ending to his narrative of the Procedural Republic, which was created, at least in part (Sandel is not a Marxist), to meet the needs of an advanced capitalist economy. In turn, the development of a global economy will spawn its own forms of political organization. Capitalism without borders spells the demise of the Procedural Republic:

> In a world where capital and goods, information and images, pollution and people, flow across national boundaries with unprecedented ease, politics must assume transnational, even global, forms, if only to keep up. Otherwise, economic power will go unchecked by democratically sanctioned political power. Nation-states, traditionally the vehicle of self-government, will find themselves increasingly unable to bring their citizens' judgments to bear on the economic forces that govern their destinies. (Sandel 1996a, 72)

A global economy demands a different kind of regulating mechanism, hence the growth of international organizations such as NAFTA and the European Union. But if, as Sandel has argued, even the nationalization of democracy disempowered citizens of the twentieth century, why should we welcome a shift of sovereignty even further away from towns and municipalities?

Nationalism could provide, although in a very limited sense, a form of identity for citizens of a nation-state. The rapid evolution of other forms of administration, such as NAFTA or the European Union, that cover very large areas with no shared language precludes this possibility, at least in the immediate future. Therefore, these larger administrative units need to foster local allegiances, as opposed to the nationalistic ones that they are combating. "Only a politics that disperses sovereignty both upward and downward can combine the power required to rival global forces with the differentiation required of a public life that hopes to inspire the allegiance of its citizens" (74). In other words, because it is impossible to turn Europe's nations' citizens into Europeans, it in necessary to make them feel a stronger alliance, for example, to their Basque, Breton, or Scottish identities. The growth of international economic, military, and economic alliances gives his theory credit, as does the reported revitalization of regional identifications across the globe. Whether these two trends really signal either an end of national sovereignty or a growth in democracy is another question. Michael Hardt and Antonio Negri's book *Empire* (2000) also describes the decline of the nation-state in the face of globalization, but the authors see the shift adversely affecting democratic possibilities. This example brings up another question about the empirical accuracy of segregating the market from both the state and civil society in our understanding of political institutions. Creating this division, as I suggested in Chapter 3, does not make political institutions immune to the demands of capitalism as much as shelter capitalism from regulation.

Finally, Benjamin Barber articulates the notion that the liberal state is inimical to communitarian citizenship. It is striking that his *Strong Democracy: Participatory Politics for a New Age* (1984), which is an extended argument for the importance of public participation, does not contain either of the words "government" or "state" in its index. Barber's book is an excellent presentation of the epistemological, psychological, and social assumptions underpinning liberal political philosophy and how they combine to create a vision that is liberal, but certainly not democratic.

Barber believes in the social constitution of identity. In his earlier work, *Liberating Feminism,* he urged feminists to turn away from an individualist model of liberation and instead embrace the need for community as an aspect of their battle. "Personal self-realization is always a function of collective identity, human liberation always conditioned by some social setting—the family, the clan, the voluntary association, the community of shared belief, the town, even the nation or the state" (Barber 1975, 14–15). Barber is undoubtedly correct, yet he fails to realize that while self-realization is conditioned by some social setting, this setting is not always an impartial one. Women's search for liberation often happens in spite of the clan, the community, the town, and the family. Barber, however, seems acutely aware of the dangers of being defined by an impersonal medium such as the bureaucratic state, but less attuned to the constraints of more intimate associations.

Barber repeatedly insists that *the state* threatens the freedom of citizens by encroaching upon their liberties and the practice of citizenship. The key to understanding his aversion to the state is his theory that representation is incompatible with freedom, equality, and morality. This is an extremely strong stance, and he seems to brook no hesitation in his objection to political representation of all kinds. He claims that representation opposes freedom

> because it delegates and thus alienates political will at the cost of genuine self-government and autonomy. . . . [R]epresentation, finally, is incompatible with social justice because it encroaches on the personal autonomy and self-sufficiency that every political order demands, because it impairs the community's ability to function as a regulating instrument of justice, and because it precludes the evolution of a participating public in which the idea of justice might take root. (Barber 1984, 146)

In response to those who have postulated that a representative democracy is the only solution in a large state, Barber replies: "The representative principle is not the salvation of democracy under conditions of mass society: it is the surrender of democracy to mass society" (251). In other words, by aggregating people into one representative, representation reinforces the anonymity of modern individuals. The problem of scale, Barber insists, can be overcome with better technologies of communication, including electronic town hall meetings and utilizing technology to improve the circulation of civic information. But this solution seems to surrender democracy to weapons of technology, not save it through their use. If representation by others is the problem, and self-representation is the solution, it is not clear how one can represent oneself in such electronic town hall meetings. Barber idealizes these technological media as transparent, but on what grounds does he assume that this form of representation does not share the problems of the other forms of representation that he rejected?

FEMINIST ANTIPATHIES TO THE LIBERAL STATE

Feminists have now thoroughly questioned any institution, practice, discourse, or representation that advances a claim of universalism. Citizenship is no exception. Since the rights and rewards of citizenship in the United States are predicated upon an abstract, a generalized, individual citizenship seems an ill-suited venue for establishing *both* women's difference *and* their equality. As Anne Phillips has noted, "It is still an open question, of course, as to whether these concerns are best approached through the concepts of citizen and citizenship, and, in a period in which feminism is exploring the problems of abstract universals, citizenship may seem a particularly unpromising avenue to pursue" (Phillips 1993, 87).

In fact, it seems that feminist critiques of both the public/private divide in liberal political thought and the white, male basis of liberal "universal" citizenship have been so successful that it is difficult to find any recent theories that entertain integrationist ideas about women and the state.[6] The anti-universalist movement in feminist theory also applies to the idea of universal citizenship. These arguments resemble Mary Ann Glendon's critique of the state as an agent of individualism. Glendon's argument is not gender specific, and she does not acknowledge that the individualist model serves some constituencies better than others.

Perhaps the most persuasive antiliberal feminist argument against the state is offered in Wendy Brown's book, *States of Injury: Power and Freedom in Late Modernity*, a damning critique of both the liberal state and those who subsume their political aspirations to this institution. Although the book contains many intricate and often compelling arguments about the nature of political freedom, political praxis, and identity, here I will focus rather narrowly on her theory of the state. Brown's central claim is that identity politics engages in a form of Nietzsche's ressentiment. Claiming redress for injuries sustained due to an identity is "a politics of recrimination that seeks to avenge the hurt even while it reaffirms it, discursively codifies it" (Brown 1995, 74). Identity politics reinforces the position of victim, rather than freeing its practitioners "to engage in something of a Nietzschean 'forgetting' of this history, in the pursuit of an emancipatory democratic project" (55). This practice not only reinforces states of injury, it also bolsters the liberal state, with disastrous consequences for the practice of freedom.

Brown calls this a "plastic cage" that "reproduces and further regulates the injured subjects it would protect" (28). Claims for redress bolster the power of the state, legitimizing it and extending the state's domain into new territory. Identity politics is complicit in what Brown characterizes as a new era of state domination: "It means that critical theory turned its gaze away from the state at the moment when a distinctly late modern form of state domination was being consolidated; transpired not through localizing and 'contracting out' its activities—in short, through what some have identified

---

6. One exception to this rule is Frances Fox Piven (1990).

as characteristically 'postmodern' techniques of power" (18). Brown echoes the communitarian distaste for rights by pointing out that they reinscribe isolation. Unlike communitarians, however, she notes that this doctrine of individualism also places blame for injuries onto the rights-bearer: "Rights may also be one of the cruelest social objects of desire dangled above those who lack them. For in the very same gesture with which they draw a circle around the individual, in the very same act with which they grant her sovereign selfhood, they turn back upon the individual all responsibilities for her failures, her condition, her poverty, her madness—they privatize her situation and mystify the powers that construct, position and buffet her" (128). The liberal state itself was the instrument of injury. Thus, in seeking comfort from the hand that slapped, identity politics obscures the nature of state and capitalist domination. Brown shadows Marx by pointing out the incomplete nature of political emancipation, taking it one step further to say that political emancipation may itself be an instrument of human oppression.

The validity of Brown's argument rests primarily on her characterization of the liberal state. Following the lead of her mentor, Sheldon Wolin, she points out the limited nature of the political life of liberalism. "A subset of this question about feminist appeals to the state concerns the politics of protection and regulation, the inescapable politics of most state-centered social policy" (169). Brown even contrasts "active *political* subjects" with "regulated, subordinated, and disciplined *state* subjects" (173).

I find Brown's argument persuasive, and her reminder that a focus on rights ignores the structures of capitalism to the detriment of those seeking to empower themselves particularly important. Her characterization of the liberal state is also accurate. But I would like to apply Brown's argument to her own text. For if liberatory politics depends upon a radical democratic practice and even imagination, then it certainly seems a worthwhile endeavor to reimagine the state. Is the state necessarily limited to regulation and protection? How can radical democratic practice change our world if it is destined to be overshadowed by an unresponsive, regulating mechanism that counters our construction of ourselves as political actors?

Brown's characterization of the state offers an important opportunity to reflect upon what exactly we mean when we talk about "the state." Often it lurks in the background of our theories as the gruesome backdrop to the crimes of modernity (and, in Brown's case, postmodernity). Brown's theory is unusual because it specifies how the state functions. But regulation and administration certainly cannot exhaust the range of possibilities for "the state." Brown's book takes significant steps toward theorizing how the state functions, as well as how it shapes both our conceptions of politics and ourselves as participants. Taking this argument to heart, it seems equally pressing to stop looking at "the state" as an amorphous structure that somehow "does" things to people rather than comprising, in the end, many different people's actions. Can we reconceptualize the state as something that can be used as the vehicle of participation instead of antithetical to it?

PARTICIPATION

One way of reconciling the dismissal of the state with an invocation of citizenship is Adrian Oldfield's distinction between citizenship as a status and citizenship as a practice (Oldfield 1990). What critics of the state really object to is the assumed status of citizenship, which embodies the exclusionary, universalistic, and institutionalizing aspects of state membership. Yet citizenship as a practice defies these norms, emphasizing the open possibilities of action in public, intermingling of difference, and seizing of self-determination. This is an appealing formulation of the problem. But doesn't one have to have the status of citizen in order to practice citizenship? Or wouldn't the practice of citizenship, as in the case of extension of suffrage or rights, tend to eventually create this status? It does not seem that these two aspects of citizenship can be entirely separated. We must conduct a more careful foray into these theories of participation in order to understand how they relate to critiques of the state.

At the core of these rejoinders to participation is a belief that action and presence are the only guarantee of adequate representation. Chantal Mouffe and Benjamin Barber offer particularly succinct and remarkably similar descriptions of what political participation accomplishes. In *The Return of the Political,* Mouffe calls for radical democracy, by which she means participatory politics. She articulates this plan as a way of "particularizing" the universal in the search for a new kind of articulation between the universal and the particular. Barber, in his description of strong democracy or participatory politics, also suggests that participation is the optimal meeting point of each person with the social framework larger than his or her self. "Strong democracy creates a public capable of reasonable public deliberation and decision and therefore rejects traditional reductionism and the fiction of atomic individuals creating social bonds ex nihilo. But it also rejects the myth of corporatism and collectivism that posits an abstract community prior to individuals and from which individuals derive their significance and purpose" (Barber 1984, 133). In other words, neither the individual nor the collective is considered prior to the other. Instead, in a mutually creating and beneficial process, citizen and collectivity create one another through participation. "Far from positing community a priori, strong democratic theory understands the creation of community as one of the chief tasks of political activity in the participatory mode. Far from positing historical identity as the condition of politics, it posits politics as the conditioner of given historical identities" (133).

Both Mouffe and Barber believe that participation provides an emancipatory bridge between the reality of our particular needs, identities, and interests, allowing entry into a larger framework of empowerment through collective action and an enlarged mentality. I will call this idea the phenomenology of participation. Participation is able to fuse the particular and universal, the singular and plural, the personal and the political, without losing the tensions between the pairings, without subsuming one half of the equation into the other. Somehow citizenship averts and foils the state's intentions, rather than affecting them. Citizenship is self-actualization, and actualization of a common body, but it is unrelated to the governmental body.

However, without attention to the conditions that make participation possible, public deliberation all too often reproduces existing inequalities rather than diffusing them. Making participation possible for everyone means being able to accommodate different viewpoints and needs and establishing a common discourse that is equally accessible to all participants. If participation is not to be a sort of flimsy scrim, making the possibility of participation a method of creating legitimacy for a continued monopoly of public opinion or space, then these two issues must be confronted.

Can everyone participate in any dialogue? Obviously not. The question then becomes, what kind of discourse is more inclusive and how can it be made the one that happens between people in public? Jürgen Habermas proposed that simple rationality is the measure of an inclusive discourse, but has been thoroughly challenged on this point (Benhabib 1992, 1996; Fraser 1997; Fleming 1993, 1997; Calhoun 1992; Meehan 1995). Habermas has now revised his earlier stance toward an emphasis upon communicative rationality, such that "the paradigm of the knowledge of objects has to be replaced by the paradigm of mutual understanding between subjects capable of speech and action" (Habermas 1995, 295–96). Some forms of "rationality" (e.g., the "male" way of viewing the world) either inadvertently or by design exclude the participation of those considered "less rational" (e.g., women, children, nonwhites). Who decides what is rational? What about those who do not follow the same method of reasoning? The apparently neutral criterion is thereby revealed to be a hurdle to participation.

On the other hand, we don't want to promote irrationality as the alternative. The tower of Babel is not a paragon of agency, self-determination, or participation. Seyla Benhabib offers a reconciliation in her essay, "Toward a Deliberative Model of Democratic Legitimacy." Here, she argues that reason or rationality can only occur out of public discourse; it cannot set the limits or boundaries of that discourse. "It is actually the deliberative process itself that is likely to produce such an outcome by leading the individual to further critical reflection on his already held views and opinions; it is incoherent to assume that individuals can start a process of public deliberation with a level of conceptual clarity about their choices and preferences that can actually result only from a successful process of deliberation" (Benhabib 1996, 71). In other words, rationality cannot be a criterion for participation—it is only the result of such participation. Benhabib is able to have the discursive public be both rational and inclusive with this turn. Invoking Hannah Arendt's concept of "enlarged mentality," Benhabib argues that the process of articulating one's viewpoint allows citizens a greater understanding of their own positions as well as those of their audience. Any person who has ever squirmed through a question-and-answer period should be able to identify the soundness of this observation. Thus, Benhabib as well looks to participation to close the gap between our internal lives and external world, helping both of them to flourish through cross-fertilization.

What about the goal of public deliberation? If consensus is the aim, wouldn't public deliberation then be a form of hegemony? If all deliberation needed to end in agreement, this would limit the possibilities for the expression of different viewpoints. The alternative, majoritarian procedure, also places unacceptable limits on public conversation, leading to head-counting and abrupt silencing of the minority opinion. Any person who is continually in the minority on public issues will soon be discouraged from participating. This seems an equally intractable yet central problem in viewing participation as the alternative to institutionalized, representative government. While some scholars say that consensus cannot be the goal because that would be participation as co-optation, it is unclear what the alternatives are. The emphasis on the phenomenology of participation often overshadows the issue of the ends of political participation. Why would participation be compelling if it never arrived at a conclusion? Inevitably, this conclusion would leave some feeling silenced or less happy than others, so participatory theories often avert the question of debate resolution. In many ways idealizing the phenomenology of participation makes it impossible to envision participation as an effective tool for change or self-governance because it obscures the goals of participation.

Mary Dietz's path-breaking article, "Context is All: Feminism and Theories of Citizenship" (1987), represents perhaps the strongest argument for a feminist reconsideration of citizenship to date. Although Dietz's concerns echo many communitarian ones, her greatest contribution to the literature is to combine an interest in democracy with a politics of feminism. She claims that the two endeavors are uniquely suited to reinforce one another.

Dietz is critical of liberal feminists who perceive the state as an instrument for and reflection of equal access for women. "To put this another way, under liberalism, citizenship becomes less a collective, political activity than an individual, economic activity—the right to pursue one's interests, without hindrance in the marketplace. Likewise democracy is tied to representative government and the right to vote rather than to the idea of the collective, participatory activity of citizens in the public realm" (Dietz 1987, 5). Dietz sees aiming for equal access as "to deal too many cards to the liberal hand."[7] Inherent to liberalism is a view of politics that cannot serve as an adequate tool of empowerment for women. "Liberalism tends towards both an understanding of power as access and a conception of citizenship as civil liberty" (6–7). Women may gain access, but access to what? The state is viewed only in negative terms. Women would not be free to act in public, as citizens, but only free to compete with one another and with men in civil society. Freedom of competition is not the same as political freedom. Dietz proposes a resurrection of citizenship, one that is clearly influenced by Arendtian notions of political liberty and action. "That conception is perhaps best called the democratic one, and it takes politics to be the collective and participatory engagement of citizens in the determination of the affairs of their community. The community may be the neighborhood, the city, the state, the region, or the nation itself. What counts is that all matters relating to the community are undertaken as 'the people's affair'" (14). This statement reflects the communitarian concern with public participation, even insofar as she refers to the location where this participation will happen as "the community." It seems what distinguishes a community in this particular literature is the ability to participate in it or to engage in self-determination in it. Similarly, Dietz sees the liberal state as

---

7. Dietz (1987, 6).

an inadequate vehicle for citizenship because it sees citizenship as a state or a status, not an activity.

> The key idea here is that citizenship must be conceived of as a continuous activity and a good in itself, not as a momentary engagement (or a socialist revolution) with an eye to a final goal or a societal arrangement. This does not mean, of course, that democratic citizens do not pursue specific social and economic ends. Politics is about such things, after all, and the debates and discussions of civic peers will necessarily center on issues of social, political, and economic concern to the community. (16)

Here Dietz breaks from her Arendtian inspiration, and insists that citizenship must encompass a full range of issues, challenging Arendt's segregation of "the social question" from the aims of citizenship (Arendt 1958, 1963). Furthermore, identity is something that can be debated and affirmed in public, meaning that feminists and citizenship are well suited to one another. Dietz claims that feminists are in a unique position to promote this kind of citizenship, as they have been practicing it in grassroots movements. Further, feminists cannot take the passive liberty offered by the liberal state and achieve political freedom. They know that liberty has to be established, it cannot be bestowed. "The democratic vision is, and feminist citizenship must be, more than this. Perhaps it is best to say that this is a vision fixed not on an end but rather inspired by a principle—freedom—and by a political activity—positive liberty. That activity is a democratic process that never ends, for it means engaging in public debate and sharing responsibility for self-government" (Dietz 1987, 16). In other words, women can only gain self-determination by avoiding the liberal state. The liberal state does not provide for self-governance; therefore achieving self-governance requires a totally different vision of political practice. Once again invoking Adrian Oldfield's categories of citizenship, we can surmise that Dietz believes that the practice of citizenship can somehow override the status of citizenship in the United States and other liberal democracies.

PARTICIPATORY STATES

I find Dietz's argument inspiring and eloquent. Yet what is to be done? I can begin going to meetings in my "community," whether I choose the neighborhood protection program, a union, or feminists against rape and war crimes. I can enter public debate; I can voice my opinion. I may even experience something akin to Arendt's "enlarged mentality." While all of this may be self-expression, self-exploration, and the development of empathy and awareness, is it self-government?

In these debates about the import of citizenship and the phenomenology of participation, the terms "public participation," "citizenship," and "self-government" have become conflated. In the United States we currently live in a representative democracy, which means that exercising self-government, by and large, is defined as voting. As the theorists I've discussed point out, voting is not substantive participation, nor is it sufficient to establish self-government. It is true that we can and should define citizenship more expansively. We can participate in governmental deliberations, and even express our opinions in public. This may change the outcome of these deliberations or it may not. But we cannot assume that public participation automatically becomes self-government given the institutional structures that function according to the principles of representativity.

I can become very active in my school, neighborhood, or bowling league, but this does not mean that I am now an entirely self-determining agent. It is as if this idea of citizenship—participation in "the community" (even the nation, which apparently can be a "community" as well)—will be so invigorating, compelling, and powerful that it will simply eclipse the stiff, blundering mechanism of the disdained liberal state. Yet such a state does exist, and will continue to exist no matter how many discussions we have about important issues, how many meetings are held to talk about town planning, women's rights, or the position of the community on any issue.

Although the liberal state may not encourage participation, and in an important sense is hostile to it, this does not imply the reverse: that the state would wither in the face of participating citizens. On the contrary, increased participation would only add legitimacy to the state that currently exists. As Sherry Arnstein established in her concise article "The Ladder of Citizen Participation" (1968), some kinds of participation are for show, are therapeutic, or bolster existing authorities. Only participation that is able to affect its own conditions is truly a form of self-governance.

I agree with the critics of the liberal state, and also with these impassioned calls for democratic regeneration. Therefore, it seems crucial to begin to think about what kind of state can encourage and accommodate a new kind of citizenship, rather than trying to envision a citizenship without a state. Even direct democracies require the institutionalized means of perseverance and administration. Why assume that participation, in and of itself, will result in self-government both without any institutional support *and* despite the presence of an elaborate governmental mechanism that follows representative principles instead?

As previously demonstrated, the debates about participation, state, and civil society are indebted to Habermas's description of an emancipatory public sphere that checks state and market forces. This schematic, in which state, civil society, and market are divided from one another, is an inheritance from liberalism. These spheres do not reflect empirical reality as much as provide a normative prescription. Let us consider an alternative configuration.

My concern is that even if we do achieve a vibrant, egalitarian, and inclusive sphere of public participation, this participation will be meaningless without institutional authority. After all, participation, even if considered a reward in itself, becomes less compelling if painful deliberation and consensus building do not result in action. Citizens may come together to debate issues that affect them in local, state, national, or international politics, but if no one is listening, the tenor of the debate must change to a discussion of the legitimacy of the government. Worldwide protests against the U.S. invasion of Iraq in 2003 were shrugged off by President George W. Bush. The result was that activists, left without the possibility of influencing government, moved to question the legitimacy of his regime. This is but one example of the frustration and stagnation that can occur when public participation and state authority are not closely linked. (I recognize that the Bush administration presents a special case, but the point stands nonetheless.)

The public and the state need not be invariably at odds with one another. While I admit that this has predominantly been the case historically, I do not believe it is an inevitable tension. John Dewey envisioned a more collaborative relationship between community, participation, and the state in *The Public and Its Problems*. His analysis of the ills of modernity foreshadows statements made seventy-five years later by communitarians: "Evils which are uncritically and indiscriminately laid at the door of industrialism and democracy might, with greater intelligence, be referred to the dislocation and unsettlement of local communities" (Dewey 1946, 212). Dewey's concern was that without face-to-face participation in local venues, what he calls "the public" will be unable to appear, or define and ultimately assert its interests. The community helps produce and shape the public, and one of the aspects of the public is that it affects and must consider those who are not directly involved in it. Dewey defines the state as "the organization of the public" (27, 33).

Dewey can serve as a corrective to contemporary theories of the state for many reasons. It is clear that the ideal of the public has been lost in the United States: in fact, between privatization, alienation and apathy, and antipathy to the state (which, after all, has the best claim to represent the public of any existing institution) we may be seeing what could be termed the nadir of the public in late modernity. Dewey's concept of the public, linked to community, also contains another important element, namely, that it represents the interests of others, not just those who compose it. Face-to-face interaction, which creates immediate mutuality, is linked to greater, more abstract communalism. While this is the aim of many thinkers who see a connection between family life or civil society and allegiance to a larger political system, there is a crucial difference between their conceptions and Dewey's. While they see community and participation as something that can exist in a universe parallel to state administration, Dewey's vision is that the state itself must be called into existence and held accountable by the public. He discards the division between civil society and the state, and the antinomy between public participation and state administration, providing a refreshing alternative to consider.

It is perhaps the most difficult task confronting a political theorist to imagine a legitimate government. Participatory democracy offers one way out of this conundrum because it presumably avoids the problem of authority through self-representation. But self-representation is only the solution to the problem of representation by others. Even direct democracies must implement methods of agenda setting, institutions of administration, procedures for discussion, and processes for changing decisions. Government requires authority. Even self-government requires a theory of authority.

Calling for participation, although an important step, has dislodged the terms of the debate and averted key questions. What would a legitimate decision-making apparatus look like? How can the state become an instrument of popular will? Isn't the first step to emphasize that it *should* be one even while we admit that it currently is not? The "state" is not as static or unalterable as it may seem. It is a complex institution with such varied guises, access points, vulnerabilities, and strengths in all of its different contexts that it is difficult to write or theorize about it. However, this inability to say definitively what the state is makes it possible to change it and use it differently. Ultimately, it is we who have the power to imagine our state.

And while the modern state may have been culled from the imaginations of early capitalists to become what it is today, economic exploitation demands that we begin to imagine the state as a powerful weapon of redistribution and justice. By accepting the segregation of the state from what is considered the realm of "freedom" we excuse its economic and social abuses. The only way to tame the behemoth is to make it our own.

5

CONSUMING COMMUNITY

Dorothy Smith has written about the interchange between text and "reality" or, rather, that which is "outside-the-text" (1999). She is critical of poststructuralist theory, claiming that it has no referent outside of itself. Without the dynamic relationship between theory and the world, theory becomes meaningless, neither guiding nor inspiring change. Smith locates the problem within the theory: poststructuralist thought creates "subject positions" instead of people who act; discourses of power seem given and unaffected by our participation. We do not so much create webs of power as live amongst them. Smith offers a corrective: a proper theory exists in dynamic relationship with the world. Text and "outside-the-text" refer to one another; through interchange, reality corrects theories, theories guide practice. This is an ideal relationship.

Up to this point, my analysis has judged theories of community in relation to existing political and social practices. But the reverse dynamic is equally important. If change does not occur from an ideal, it is tempting to assume we need to somehow "fix" the idea. Looking at political imagination as an interchange between ideal and material demands that we consider how theory fares in the world. What if the world, not just the theory, is to blame when the relationship between theory and practice breaks down?

Contemporary life in the United States teaches us to be consumers: to relate to one another, to find ourselves, and to satiate desire through consumption. Our ideals can become materialized through commodification. If our desire is for sociality, the market offers a plethora of options that respond to it. How does this particular way of relating our imagination and desires in the world affect our ability to realize ideals of community?

CELEBRATION, FLORIDA

The 1998 film *The Truman Show* is an updated version of a recurring theme in American folklore. Truman, the heroic individual played by Jim Carrey, battles valiantly to free himself from an amoral community. Ed Harris is the patriarch who sacrifices Truman's life on the twin altars of satellite television and product endorsements in order to achieve his own hyper-individualistic dream of ultimate success—to be the producer of the most popular television show in history. Truman's escape from the surveillance of the town via sailboat brings the film to a crescendo reminiscent of Hemingway's "The Old Man and the Sea," his spirit winning over the unnatural elements that are ruled by Father Nature/Big Brother.

In the Hollywood version of the story, once Truman finds out that he is living in a controlled environment he wants to escape. But the inside joke of *The Truman Show* is that it was filmed in Seaside, Florida—a town hailed as the model of new urbanist development with a waiting list for those who want to move in. New urbanist architects and developers strategize that we all long for the days of small towns, front porches, and pedestrian lifestyles, and thus far, the market has proved them right. Hence we are faced with two contradictory narratives: is what lurks beneath the American breast a desire for individual freedom or the comforts of community?

After studying theorist after theorist trying to articulate the difficult balance between individual autonomy and community membership, I suspect that one way to achieve a balance between individual and community may be in the gap between the ideal community of one's mind and the real communities of experience. Pat philosophical formulas—"In some categories the community's needs come before the individual's" or "The individual cannot exist a priori to the community"—do not balance individual and community the same way that our psychic juggling of real and ideal communities can. To those who might reply that I am ascribing too much sophistication to the average citizen, I need only point out that consumer capitalism and commodity fetishism provide my model here. If there is anything that Americans have mastered, it is how to generate boundless desire for gratification, without ever achieving it or expecting to. We know that the gap between promise and acquisition is eternal, yet rather than frustrating us, it only leaves us coming back for more. With this in mind I began to ask what consumer capitalism and commodity fetishism can tell us about the political theory of community, and what the function of the gap between real and ideal communities achieves.

This proposition immediately contests the cardinal rule of theories of community, adopted from Ferdinand Tönnies's groundbreaking work (1957). According to this model we tend to delineate community through reference to its opposite—impersonal, busy society. Community, or *Gemeinschaft*, the location of our most authentic identity, is necessarily small scale. Agrarian economies and small towns are inextricably tied to this model. This realm is under vicious attack by *Gesellschaft*—society—which threatens to turn us all into interchangeable automatons and destroy the world built on a personal scale. Capitalism has wrought *Gesellschaft*. Globalization is just the latest step in the destruction of the local and distinctive. While I have perhaps overdrawn these categories, there is an intuitive distinction here that most can follow, and perhaps even sympathize with. However, I believe this dichotomous understanding hampers our ability to apprehend how community functions in our world. Capitalism and community have come to be intricately connected and maintaining this conceptual schema that categorically divides the two occludes this fact.

The goal here is to explore these two propositions. First, there is a serious disjunction between the ways we imagine communities and how we experience them. Second, today communities are not havens from economics, but instead are profoundly influenced by capitalism. I combine these two assertions in my analysis of the town of Celebration, Florida, noting that consumer capitalism is intricately involved in our experience of community, and indeed provides for a reconciliation of our imagined and physical communities.

In the United States, people pay extra to move to new urbanist towns that are fabricated to provide their residents with the rigid, controlled environment of the small towns of yore. Until four years ago, Seaside, Florida, was the largest new urbanist development in the United States.[1] Now that honor belongs to Celebration, Florida—the town that Disney built adjacent to its themed universe in Orlando. This chapter is neither an expose of Celebration nor a complete examination of the town, its planning, and its history.[2] Some readers may counter that examining Celebration is choosing an easy target—anything with Disney attached is bound to be the exception rather than the rule. Indeed, Celebration is a unique case. But I believe it

---

1. The two architects of Seaside, Florida, Andreas Duany and Elizabeth Plater-Zyberk, were consulted about Celebration's design, although they are not credited with the final product (Rymer 1996). The towns seem very similar to one another, although in my opinion Seaside has far more interesting housing, while Celebration's downtown is more unusual. I am not the only person to recognize the similarities between the two towns. In a story for the *New York Times,* a correspondent who lives in Celebration reported that a tourist stopped his wife on the street in Celebration to ask, "Where is Truman?"(Franzt 1998).

2. For a complete history of Celebration and the Disney Corporation, see Foglesong (2003). Two reporters and one academic moved to Celebration and wrote books about their experiences, Franzt and Collins (1999) and Ross (1999).

is uniquely able to draw attention to the dynamic that is present in many new developments and redevelopments in this country. The National Association of Realtors has categorized "community" as one of the prime selling points on any property. Celebration only exists because there is a ready-made market for community in this country. And as in any enterprise that it undertakes, Disney aims to capture the largest market share. I have seen little resistance to the marketing of community in the United States, and even less to the "new traditionalist" ideas about neighborhood development that have become fashionable in the last ten years.[3] But as soon as Disney became involved, suddenly everyone seemed skeptical about building a community from scratch. I believe what makes Celebration unique is the amount of resistance that it has encountered, not its methods for building and marketing community.

Celebration is not the easy target it initially seems to be. In fact, Disney works very hard to provide community in Celebration, unlike most of the developments that claim to do so. I am not going to criticize Disney's failures. What is more interesting for the purposes of this project is the character of Disney's successes. People that live in Celebration seem to feel like they do live in "a real community." Rather than discounting these statements as false consciousness, I want to consider what it is about Celebration that provides this "sense of community."

THE LANDSCAPE OF COMMUNITY

When my husband and I visited Celebration, Florida, our first shock was seeing the unattractive sprawl along the highway that borders the town. Surprisingly, none of the snide articles already published on Celebration mentioned or included a picture of the strip skyline that is sometimes visible within the development. The presence of Disney theme parks in Orlando has made it a strip megalopolis comparable to Las Vegas, as everyone tries to build something to catch a few of the dollars fluttering out of tourist wallets. Just across the street from Celebration, there is a huge water park, outlet stores, and a gigantic restaurant called Arabian Nights (!)

---

3. The notable exception is in city planning and in architectural schools. There has been an extended debate whether such new principles of urban development really do promote communal interaction, or whether they are just suburbs with "a human face." For an instructive contrast between ideas of new urbanism and a more intensely communally oriented approach to housing, see McCamant and Durrett (1988).

that features scantily clad ladies in vaguely Orientalist outfits riding large Arabian stallions and performing death-defying tricks during your dinner. It should not be too surprising that entering Celebration provides a welcome respite for the eyes. Ironically, Disney provides a haven from its own sprawl.

This was confusing, as I had come prepared to despise Celebration. Perhaps this was due to the articles I had read about the place. The press had been having a field day with Celebration,[4] publishing snickering articles with titles such as "A Mouse in the House" (Rothchild 1995), "The Mickey House Club" (Ross 1997), and "It's A Small Town After All" (*Economist* 1995). I wanted to see signs of phoniness, insincerity, and totalitarianism everywhere. I discovered the visual metaphor for my assumptions in the child-care center located next to the Corporate Plaza, called Celebration Place. Here, a flimsy facade of a Victorian house was attached to a low-grade aluminum building. Looking at the building, I realized that this is what I had expected—a facade of traditionalism to camouflage seemingly down-and-dirty money grubbing.

But why did I, and so many other intellectuals, seemed to be so offended at the idea of Celebration? There was no comparable outcry against any other "new urbanist" development. Obviously, the fact that *Disney* is behind Celebration is what is scary. Disney has always sold fantasy. But it was fantasy that allowed an escape from the mundane and everyday: films, books, even Disneyland are unmistakably part of the world of imagination. But here the Disney Imagineers are offering us fantasy as real life.[5] We can buy it and move in permanently.

Andrew Ross, Professor of American Studies at New York University, lived in Celebration for six months and was disturbed at Disney's profit mongering in the face of cherished American ideals about traditional communities. The presence of a profiting corporate monster leads Ross to label the town and its residents as a distortion of the American dream: his book is titled *The Celebration Chronicles: Life, Liberty, and the Pursuit of Property Values in Disney's New Town* (1999). But I believe it is more interesting to consider the ways that community and capitalism interact with one another. While ultimately this discussion may paint a more pessimistic view

---

4. In fact, Herbert Muschamp (1998) in a piece about Disney architecture commented that "smart people don't like Celebration."
5. Disney Imagineering has been in charge of the Celebration project from the beginning. Even now public notices for bids on property are posted on letterhead with Disney Imagineering embossed on it.

than Ross's desire for a pure community, it also seems a necessary innovation. Communities don't magically exist outside of the consumer culture that permeates all other facets of our lives: the question is, how have they come to coexist? Once we understand how we consume community today, it is possible to consider the alternatives.

The emblem of Celebration is a perfect example of the Disney Imagineers Team at work. The graphic, which serves as the town's seal, is a little girl with pigtails flying in the wind, riding her bike and followed by a dog, framed underneath a mature oak tree. It is replicated so frequently, and in such odd locales, that the emblem, which is supposed to signal a down-home feeling, actually becomes surreal. The seal is in the middle of a fountain, on gates, walls, all street signs, and most eerily, made into a three-dimensional cast-iron figure that hangs over Main Street. In the end, the symbol has the effect of making the town seem less real and more like a theme park of a town whose image must be continually reinforced by the symbol that indicates "This *is* a small town!" Not to be daunted by the small matter of climate, Celebration city managers recognized that a white Christmas is an important component of every small-town experience. So they arranged for an hourly snowfall on the downtown streets of Celebration during the 2003 holiday season. Once again, meeting the steep expectations for an ideal small town experience can sometimes lead to an absurd contortion of the given environment.

Yet even this jaded visitor had to admit that the architecture downtown was the most interesting yet sensible around Orlando. The real estate agent with whom we spoke boasted that seven years of planning preceded breaking ground. The array of architects who helped to plan Celebration is a virtual who's who of contemporary architecture: Robert Stern, who is on the board of Celebration, designed the Health Campus and developed the Master Plan for the town,[6] Robert Venturi and Denise Scott-Brown designed the town bank. Michael Graves planned the post office, and Philip Johnson the town hall, whose meeting room is called Johnson Hall. Cesar Pelli's movie theater is almost majestic—a fitting tribute to the entertainment millions that helped to fund the whole endeavor.

Celebration is different from other large suburban developments in five ways. First, Disney planners have tried to build a multi-use development. They began constructing the downtown area and school before they built

---

6. Although supposedly "smart people don't like Celebration" (see note 4 above), Stern was promoted to be head of the Yale School of Architecture after his Celebration endeavor.

houses. Celebration is intended to be a self-sufficient development, with school, work, shopping, entertainment, and health care located within its borders. An extremely tall white fence, designed to invoke a traditional picket fence, surrounds the entire town. It is just tall enough to be prohibitive, yet from the car it seems welcoming. The downtown area only has four or five blocks of stores, but the limited size seems natural nonetheless because it is bordered by an artificial lakefront park.

A large parking lot segregates the downtown shops and restaurants from the expensive estate homes, providing both a natural buffer and some indication of the amount of traffic developers were expecting. A brochure prominently displayed in all retail stores proclaims "Celebration, Florida: You don't have to live here to love it." All of the stores are rather expensive; for example, the diner that charges roughly ten dollars per plate. Perhaps most disconcerting to me was the grocery store / convenience market that sold complete, "homemade" meatloaf and roast turkey dinners in microwaveable plastic containers. Also prominently displayed were prepackaged school lunch sets for children. These items prompted me to ask, is this what a traditional lifestyle means? The brochure I picked up hawks "The Town of Celebration blends upscale shopping and down-home ambiance for an experience enjoyed by residents and visitors alike." The newest apartment complexes downtown house day spas, so residents can be guaranteed the old-fashioned comforts of the Roman Spa combined with the newest in therapeutic treatments.

The second aspect that distinguishes Celebration from other developments is the wide range in price and style of dwellings. Apartments and townhouses surround the downtown except for the edge with the parking lot, and provide a surprisingly nice atmosphere that is urban in feel, similar to Georgetown or Alexandria near Washington, D.C. Apartments are built over storefronts, violating an honored contemporary zoning principle, instead copying towns of the past. Buyers of larger houses have the option of putting in garage apartments. All of these decisions are intended to create a genuinely diverse community of people with varying levels of income. Theoretically, a college student, a pensioner, a single mother, and a millionaire could all live in Celebration together in dwellings appropriate to their lifestyle needs and income levels.

The goal of economic diversity, however, is not actually met. During our visit, the town hall bulletin board displayed advertisements for some of these garage apartments. These one-bedroom apartments rent for an astounding average of $1,000 per month, and some luxury apartments rent for $2,400 per month. Clearly, college students, struggling widows, and single mothers just propelled into the minimum-wage work force would not be able to afford these apartments. These rental rates were well above the Orlando market rate. The other prohibitive element is the dearth of public transportation in Celebration. Of course one can walk around town,[7] but getting to a full grocery store or pharmacy requires a car.

The third element that sets Celebration apart from other developments is its new urbanist design. I find this term confusing, because there is very little that seems urban about these designs: the movement tends to model itself on mythical small towns rather than, say, Greenwich Village. Revealingly, this style is also called neotraditionalist. The primary goal of new urbanism is to create more public space, encourage communal interaction, and design with the needs of people instead of automobiles in mind. Homes in Celebration follow the new prescriptions for community planning, including a requisite front porch, garages neatly hidden so as not to disrupt the face of the house, and houses situated close to the sidewalk (Kunstler 1996). There is also a plethora of "public space" in Celebration—there seems to be a park, swing set, and clubhouse structure on every block.

Celebration provides an interesting lesson in the difficulties of trying to design public space. The rows of townhouses create a wall along the sidewalk that has the effect of creating an outdoor room, a public space on a human scale (Cullen 1961; Clay 1973, 1987). I found this area of town to be the most successful at creating a sense of place, interchange, and comfort. Unfortunately, Celebration's downtown is not as successful in this endeavor, since the main street is too wide for there to be an intimate feel to the street; in the open space pedestrians feel vulnerable, exposed, and conspicuous. In Celebration Village, an emphasis upon public space actually works against the developers in creating an atmosphere on a human scale. Wide parkways in the middle of streets, parks at the end, and a meandering grid design that prevents direct access to the next street make Celebration more auto than pedestrian friendly.

The lot sizes for houses are small, but the abundance of public spaces around the houses is supposed to compensate for this fact. The current low price point in Celebration is a "garden home"—an amusing misnomer since their lot areas do not contain enough space to have even the tiniest

---

7. Yet the distance from the new houses being built to the downtown area is over a mile. The real estate agent recommended that we drive because the heat is too intense for such a walk. So even within Celebration, a car is necessary for most residents.

of gardens. The retail prices of homes in Celebration range from garden homes at $280,000 to $320,000, to estate homes that start at $800,000. Townhomes with 1,400 square feet sell for $250,000. Interestingly, the sale of garden homes is especially brisk; one real estate agent told us that they sold all fifty-six designated lots for garden homes in fifty-six days.

These prices are very well above prices in comparable developments around Orlando, but, Disney argues, you get much more than a house in Celebration. As their billboard advertises, "Shop for a house, buy a town!" This brings me to the fourth element that distinguishes Celebration: the infrastructural investment that only one of the wealthiest corporations in the world could provide. Certain aspects of Celebration are remarkably close to Walt Disney's original vision for his Experimental Prototype Community of Tomorrow (EPCOT). For example, Disney's EPCOT was intended to be a town with 20,000 residents—the same number that Celebration will have when building is complete. The film we viewed at the real estate office in Celebration began with Walt Disney's introduction of EPCOT, thereby invoking the authority of a great, deceased patriarchal founder. Disney wanted his town "to be a showcase for American industry and research, schools, cultural and educational opportunities" (Mosley 1986, 287). In accordance with this aspect of the original vision, homes in Celebration are all wired into a computer network, and school and health facilities are touted as state of the art.

Disney poured money into a model school and teaching academy that serves as a pedagogical training and research center for the entire country. Class sizes are relatively small, although not as small as I expected, at twenty-five students per teacher. Disney invested in education in order to make investing in Celebration more attractive. Ironically, the school has been the largest issue of contention in the town's brief history. Some parents were unhappy with the school's innovative curriculum, which allowed students to pace themselves, had multi-age classrooms, and used innovative (if controversial) teaching methods such as the whole-language approach to reading (Burstein 1995). Recently, however, the school has been reorganized according to more traditional teaching philosophies. The school does not assign grades; instead teachers provide "narrative assessments." The principal of the school in Celebration boasts, "This is a place where nobody fails" (Pollan 1997).

The other advantage that Celebration wields in terms of infrastructural investment is a hospital with a prestigious cancer research unit, and an equally large "health campus." All residents are able to use the "health campus," one of the world's largest and best-equipped gyms. Disney argues that it is providing health care for all stages of life, including the increasingly recognized preventative aspect. Obviously, the hospital is meant to attract wealthy retirees, just as the school serves as a magnet for younger families concerned with pupil achievement. These infrastructural investments seem to be Celebration's most unequivocal advantage and attraction.

A final aspect of Celebration sets it apart from other real estate developments: although it is unmistakably a development for the well-to-do, it does not emphasize its exclusivity. The variation in housing price points is supposed to indicate the true inclusivity of Celebration as a community. This corresponds to our common rhetoric about community. Community is something that is not supposed to involve money; in fact, it is ideally a respite from the pressures of market and status. Therefore, not mentioning the vulgarities of income or returns on investment is an integral part of the presentation of Celebration as a "real community." But the vision and the reality are quite distinct from one another upon close examination.

The realtors with whom we spoke were extremely careful not to mention money, income, or the word "exclusive" in their presentation of Celebration. In fact, they acted as though buying a house was not an economic endeavor at all. They asked my husband and I how many bedrooms we would need, rather than what our price range would be. The homes with the lowest price points—the only ones we could afford even with our hypothetical dual-academic salary—were tiny: two or three bedrooms, two baths, and a large combination kitchen, family room, and dining room area. These so-called garden homes were not pitched as affordable; rather the agent emphasized they were for people like us who didn't have the time to take care of a yard. (We had not said anything about being busy.) Conveniently, this sales pitch simultaneously averts pointing out that we would have been struggling to buy into the community and accounts for the unexpected lack of a yard around a suburban house.

Remarkably, Celebration considers itself an "inclusive" community even though the prices for its homes are very well above the median price for homes in Orlando, which is $98,500. Home prices in Celebration have been estimated to be from 10 to 40 percent above the price of comparable homes in the Orlando real estate market. Regardless, when Disney first proposed Celebration, the corporation told local officials that it would provide affordable housing for their employees. Affordable housing in Orlando has become a major problem, as Walt Disney World and many of the service industries that cluster around it pay minimum wages to their employees.

Furthermore, Disney relies heavily upon part-time and temporary help to staff its parks during peak attendance periods.

Celebration does seem to have many dual-income families; the only people we saw out in the middle of the day in Celebration were a veritable army of landscapers. We only saw one woman out with a stroller. However, the people who work in town cannot afford to live there, not even the real estate agent who nonetheless urged us to "Come and join us" as we left the sales office. Andrew Ross indicates that tight resources are a common problem in town. Many families stretched beyond their means to be able to live in Celebration and belong to "a real community." Sadly, the need to take an extra job or work longer hours to make house payments makes it impossible to participate in events in town. Ross writes that "I had been in town for only a few days when I first heard the Celebration mantra that mostly everyone here was 'house-rich and cash-poor'" (Ross 1999, 32). He also reported that it was not unusual to see homes that were without inside furnishings because all available funds had been spent for the mortgage.

Although the rhetoric of Celebration, and of community more broadly, is often inclusive, it is interesting to consider the small indications that do establish the boundaries of any community. In the case of a social club, for instance, pointed questions, lack of friendliness, or cold shoulders tell us when we are not wanted. Towns carry the architectural equivalents of these signals. What was surprising in Celebration was that they were not very hard to find, even though the town was designed as a "new urbanist" community. A first example is the white fences that surround the town, which invoke aspects of both farm fences and white picket fences. But standing next to one reveals that it is quite tall and prohibitive. The fence simultaneously acts as a welcoming gesture to those who are in cars and a serious obstacle to those who are on foot.

Similarly, the security signs that dot the front of almost every yard give the clear impression that intruders are not welcome. Because the town remains such an isolated enclave, such security signs also signal a distrust of strangers. Since many homes stand empty, incredibly, homes that *are* occupied often have a sign indicating such and order no trespassing. This is undoubtedly due to the masses of prospective home buyers who visit the town as though its entirety is an open model home. These signs also draw attention to the fact that Celebration still looks uninhabited, like it is waiting for residents, although thousands have already arrived.

Perhaps our strangest experience of Celebration was watching the video testament from current residents that is shown to prospective home buyers in the real estate office. The ten-minute video is a compilation of interviews with different residents. Repeatedly, they all attest to the fact that living in Celebration is "*like* living in a real community." These residents stress that the town's inhabitants have "the same goals for our children" and "share common values." Residents indicate that they know all of their neighbors, and that there is "a sense of peace" in the town provided by the pastel colors of the architecture. These sentiments are repeated by those that were interviewed for articles on Celebration as well. One resident claimed, "We wanted to re-create what we had in Canada. Feeling safe, walking down the street or to a movie, letting your kids bike around town. That's what we had when we were growing up, and that's what we wanted for our kids. We bought into that dream. If we weren't here, we'd be back in Canada" (Phillips and Lorrayne 1997). Similarly, another woman reports, "This place is about creating community" and "we hear people from all over the country saying 'I've been looking for a place like Celebration for a long time, and I didn't think I could ever find it'" (Kroloff 1997).

A striking moment in the video presentation is a discussion about health and security. In talking about the Health Campus, the official Disney voice that narrates the video proclaims that Walt wanted his town to be "the healthiest community in the world." The slippage between a robust community life and the health of the individuals that belong to it seems intentional. This comment is immediately followed by more than one resident who speaks about living in Celebration as possessing "internal security." One usually associates the idea of security with protection from the outside world. But what does internal security mean? Here residents seem to invoke a particular kind of psychological comfort from residency in Celebration, also talking about the calming effect of the town's pastel colors. Clearly, there is a psychology of community at work that needs exploration.

THE MYTH OF COMMUNITY

In his book *The Uses of Disorder: Personal Identity and City Life*, Richard Sennett proposes that the search for community in this country is the result of stymied personal psychological development. As the individual becomes an adolescent, she becomes more concerned with forming an identity independent of family membership. The result of this desire to find oneself in adolescence is what Sennett terms "a defensive pattern." "The result of this defensive pattern is to create in people a desire for a purification of terms in which they see themselves in relation to others. The enterprise involved is an attempt to build an image or identity that coheres, is unified, and filters out threats in social experience" (Sennett 1971, 9). In other words, as we become uncertain about who we are, we become increasingly anxious to avoid challenges to our preconceptions and assumptions from the outside world. Sennett believes that most individuals in today's society do not ever overcome this adolescent urge. Quite the contrary, he argues that we have started to construct our social institutions as a way of prolonging our emotional adolescence, our need for purity. Sennett's position stands in contrast to Iris Marion Young, who argues that the expulsion of difference is an inevitable part of "the logic of identity" (Young 1990, chap. 1). Sennett believes that the drive for purity is a stage of adolescence that tragically remains the standard operating principle for adults as well.

Although the observation about the defensive posture of adolescence has been made by others, most notably Erik Erikson (1958), Sennett's book is unique in linking this behavior with the desire for community in the United States.

> That the adolescent process of making an identity of coherence has a social character can be seen in such areas as adolescent career choice, sexual identity, and the pretensions of emotionless competence. But a communal structure that is built out of desires for purity in adolescence means something more: when the purification desires of a large number of people succeed and become dominant in their lives, it would only be natural for these men to try and mold society in their own image, so that the structure of society would be organized to encourage and to codify this peculiar escape from painful disorder. (Sennett 1971, 25)

Sennett argues that these structures built out of a desire for purity are embodied in the quest for what he terms "purified community." The purified community is the idea that everyone living in a community is similar and that all exist synchronously. Sennett is careful to emphasize that this purified community is only a myth, however. As evidence, he cites studies by David Reisman and Maurice Stein, as well as Florian Znanick, that demonstrated that "purified communities" were not built around shared experience, but rather were "an act of will" (32–33). These communities were based upon the *belief* that everyone was the same and lived in total agreement with one another. This belief in communal homogeneity often belies the actual levels of discordance and difference that exist within communities.

Sennett argues that the myth of purified community only works because it is the expression, en masse, of personal adolescence and the fear of being challenged by the outside world. The myth of purified community acts as a buffer between ourselves and our environments in two ways. First, the myth of community becomes more pronounced during periods of change and unrest, as "the desire to define a common 'us' so that men may forge a common bulwark for themselves against disorder" (34). This urge to create a space of safety and stability defined in opposition to the chaos of change elsewhere has been noted by other observers as well (Reagon 1983; Young 1990). But the myth of community also helps to protect the members of the community from other members, not just those outside it. Sennett proposes that "what is distinctive about this mythic sharing in communities is that people feel they belong to each other, and share together, because they are the same . . . the 'we' feeling, which exposes a desire to be similar, is a way for men to avoid the necessity of looking deeper into one another" (Sennett 1971, 39). Telling oneself that everyone in one's community is just like oneself provides a compelling logic for not needing to know these others in the community. Additionally, this belief works as a psychological screen that helps to obscure any information that indicates that members of the community are indeed different from these expectations. Sennett's theory clearly points out how the myth of purity works to isolate individuals from both the people outside of the community and other people in it.

Sennett further asserts that the myth of purified community tends to thrive in affluent social groups because material resources allow individuals to sustain the myth of community more effectively. Material abundance helps to maintain the myth by providing the resources necessary to police the boundaries of the community, keeping all "undesirables" out. (Hence one explanation of the proliferation of "gated communities" across in the United States.) Second, wealth makes individuals more self-reliant. Neighbors do not have to share baby-sitters or tips on yard maintenance, or pool their labor if everyone can hire a nanny, gardener, and house painter. Lack of actual contact means that the myth of similarity can be maintained more easily (47–49).

Sennett ultimately charges that the myth of purified community "reveals the marks of adolescence on the community process" (36). However, while the desire for purity may drive the search for a mythic community, it cannot fully explicate the form that communities take and how they are maintained. What is valuable about Sennett's theory is his apt observation that often the ways communities are imagined and the ways they exist are radically at odds with one another. Furthermore, his theory offers an explanation for why we are compelled to construct an image of mythic community even if we can never live in one.

Disney's Celebration illustrates that the image of community is more important than the personal experience of community. However, only models of consumption can explain the phenomenon of why Celebration residents are satisfied by their small-town facsimile and why living somewhere that is "like a community" is preferable to living in a community. Sennett's work provides insight into the psychological roots of our consumer desires and our motivation to overlook reality in favor of fantasy. Consumer capitalism provides the model of eternal nonfulfillment and can account for the gap between the promise and the delivery of the product.

Most Celebration residents fervently believe that there is something different about Celebration and that they are living in "a real community." Even the *New York Times* correspondent reported that he and his wife "were pleased to find a degree of community spirit" in the town (Franzt 1998). Yet to this observer, there was very little that ultimately distinguished Celebration from other suburbs. The people were no more friendly than folks in other towns. Just like any other suburb, there were virtually no pedestrians. All of the front porches, so faithfully built, were conspicuously empty. People talked about being involved in Celebration, but I had to wonder what kind of involvement they meant. After all, governance of the town was controlled by the Disney Corporation until 2003. Now homeowners hold a majority of seats in the homeowners' district, but Disney retains the largest share. It is not an option to involve oneself politically in Celebration and to chart its future; this community is not an exercise in collective self-determination. Instead, these people were involved in the story of Celebration—the story that they lived in the only "real community" in the United States. Disney does not have to enforce the myth that Celebration is a real community; it only has to try to keep this dream from being dislodged. As the General Manager of Disney Development remarked, "We're giving people exactly what they've asked for" (*Economist* 1995).

I emphasize that this is a story because it is clear that most residents of Celebration relish the myth of purified community. This is a common story in American marketing, a point to which I shall return shortly. It is striking that the story does not necessarily have to be true. For example, one of the most commonly mentioned features of living in Celebration was the fact that there was increased security from knowing all of your neighbors. Yet ninety percent of the houses in Celebration had home security systems. Rather than indicating a feeling of security, the presence of an alarm system seems to show that one neither feels secure nor trusts one's neighbors' eyes as much as an electronic one to guard the home; and further, completely averts the necessity of knowing one's neighbors at all.

Another example of the distinction between the community as it is imagined versus how it exists is manifested in the white picket fences that encircle the yards of the smaller homes. The picket fences invoke traditionalism and the spaciousness of the old homestead. But behind the picket fences are often only narrow strips of grass approximately twelve square feet. No child could play ball, no family could gather, no event could be held in this space. The only practical use one can imagine is that these yards could double as playpens. The description of houses with white picket fences pervades the Celebration literature, invoking the dream, signaling a past era—yet in reality woefully short of the promise. No residents that have been interviewed complained about this aspect of living in Celebration. In fact, remarkably few residents seem to have had their dream of community dislodged by the reality of living in it.

This is not to say that the illusion of community is able to provide everything it promises. As the promotional video for Celebration indicates, an important part of our vision of community is that when we live in one we are secure. But it is difficult even for Disney to provide its residents a feeling of "internal" security if it is not something that originates from within. The vision of community cannot overtake the search for it. As Sennett indicates, since we are driven to construct community out of our insecurities, "finding" the mythic community does not overcome that insecurity: it only seems to enable it to prosper. To illustrate the struggle between the illusion of security and the insecurity that propels the search for community, consider the comments by one Celebration resident. This woman works at the movie theater and lives in a downtown apartment only fifty yards away. When she walks home at night she claims to feel safe. This is not surprising given the short distance, the continual police presence on Main Street, and the geographical isolation of Celebration from less "desirable" parts of Orlando. Despite all of these factors, her belief in her safety wavers, as demonstrated by this revealing protest: "I really believe I am safe, and I don't think it's just an illusion created by the company" (Ross 1997).

CONSUMPTION AND THE CONTRADICTIONS OF COMMUNITY

Although Sennett aptly points out that affluent communities are able to secure their myths, he does not extend his analysis to include a consideration of how capitalism works to sustain the contradictions of community. The images used to market products promise a lifestyle often radically at odds with the product being sold. Take, for example, a telephone commercial. While a popular slogan of the early 1980s was to "reach out and touch someone," the telephone effectively makes it possible to *avoid* physical contact with those to whom you are speaking. One long-distance commercial features a large family gathering to pass the phone from aunt to grandmother to nephew so that the one person who must be apart from the family can in effect "be there" as well. The commercial allows *the viewer* to experience the family gathering without having to be there. We can have the image of family togetherness, without having to endure the reality—noise, embarrassing questions, a pedantic uncle, misbehaving children, quarrels over how to cook the dinner, who is to do the dishes, and so forth.

This is but one example of how images of sociality, togetherness, or community pervade the world of advertising. Small towns, front porches, a grandmother in a rocker, a white house behind a picket fence—these images are planted in our collective unconscious by the advertising executives of the world. This is not to say that when we buy the products being offered behind all of these images, we actually think that we are buying community, sociality, or small-town America. Consumers are much savvier than that. One of the attractions of the myth of community in advertising is precisely that it is recognized as the eternally unachievable, thus leading to never-ending desire. We become accustomed to maintaining desire for particular images, never expecting to achieve them, hence comments about Celebration such as "I've been looking for a place like Celebration for a long time, and I didn't think I could ever find it" (Kroloff 1997). In this sense, the project of Celebration is dangerous because it actually tries to deliver the unattainable. The quandary then becomes how to keep consumer desire from being disappointed by the delivered product. In short, it is necessary to have the desire itself occlude the reality.

The signifiers of community, picket fences, front porches, a little girl on a bike, create the desire for "community." Being surrounded by these signifiers simultaneously evokes and satisfies our created desire. Desire and signifier become a mutually reinforcing cycle, without the necessity of a signified. Consider, for example, this statement made about the potential experience of the town of Celebration made by one of its creators, Peter Rummel, President of Disney Design and Development. "Hopefully, someday you'll be able to walk down a street or sit someplace and kind of close your eyes and get some comfort that there are people who have been here before you, that this feels like a place that has a tradition, even though it doesn't" (Rymer 1996).

Looking at the dynamics of consumption gives an indication of how as a culture we have come to be able to experience myths without believing them. Understanding the extent to which Celebration is able to sustain its myth of community requires yet another point of analysis. Maintaining the myth requires that the reality of living there does not overly intrude upon the consciousness of its residents. The story of "real community" must remain the dominant narrative, and in order to do so it must be the primary connection that is shared by those in Celebration. This is not to say that shared experiences would inevitably be bad, only that any experience at all would begin to push the residents' ability to recite the uncomplicated narrative of community. Therefore, in order to maintain Celebration as "the real community" its residents say it is (and therefore justify the greater real estate prices) Disney must make sure that nothing can fatally disrupt the story of community.

THE POLITICS OF CELEBRATION

The cost of maintaining a place like Celebration with its self-conscious "community" is actually quite high. This price is paid by those who do not live in the town as well as the residents. The resources needed to create this "real community" have drained the surrounding area indirectly and directly. Celebration has inherited a troubled relationship with the greater Orlando economy from its parent, the Disney Corporation. In order to understand the town's unique economic and political status, it is necessary to provide a brief history of Disney's activities and history in the Orlando area.

In the early 1960s, Walt Disney sent a number of ghost buyers to purchase enormous tracts of swamp land for the cost of $200 an acre. Disney later insisted that this secrecy was necessary because he wanted to buy a much larger area than the land for Disneyland in Anaheim, California, which was hemmed in by other businesses and could not expand. Furthermore, he knew that as soon as word that Disney was building another theme park was released, property values in Orlando would skyrocket. As a result, he bought 30,000 acres next to Orlando at low prices, ensuring that Walt Disney World would be able to expand indefinitely.

But before Disney commenced construction, he obtained an unprecedented guarantee from the Orlando government and Florida legislature. In exchange for building what would undoubtedly become a major tourist attraction in Orlando and attracting millions of tourist dollars, all local control of the property had to be ceded to the Disney Corporation (Foglesong 2003). More specifically,

> For the first time in Florida history, control over all the territory to be included in the future Disney World was ceded to the owners. The new park would become what amounted to a self-governing community, with its own laws and police services, hospitals, health and all necessary maintenance departments, plus a special tax rate; and no outside authority would be allowed to enter its territory without an invitation from the owners nor would its finances or affairs be subject to control by the state. (Mosley 1986, 282–83)

Long before privatization and minimal government became a strategy to attract investors, Disney and the Florida government struck the bargain that foreshadowed the coming era of business and government relations. In addition to becoming the sole authority over this installation of the Magic Kingdom, Disney was also exempted from contributing to the local tax base.

The loss of tax payments was supposed to be more than compensated for by tourist revenues and the boom in local employment. Although tourist dollars have certainly arrived as promised, Disney tends to hire part-time workers at minimum wages. This creates a tremendous demand for low-income housing as well as an undeniable need for social services that aid families with lower incomes. Thus, Osceola County, one of the two counties that the Disney property spans, must help the workers underpaid by Disney without the benefits of sharing in the Disney profits.

The Disney corporation developed a rather complicated system for maintaining a formally democratic form of government while simultaneously exerting total control over its property. Disney established two different townships on the property, Bay Lake and Lake Buena Vista, which have a total of forty-three residents. All of these residents are Disney employees at the supervisory level. The townships hold elections regularly, and the representatives unanimously vote in favor of ceding the powers of the municipalities to the Reedy Creek Improvement District (RCID). Thus, the townships willingly abdicate all powers of taxation, zoning, and planning to the RCID. Membership in the Reedy Creek Improvement District is also determined by formally democratic procedures: all landowners get a vote, where one acre of property equals one vote for RCID elections. Of course, Disney owns 98 percent of the land, and is therefore able to select who sits on the board of Reedy Creek, namely, Disney executives.

After Michael Eisner took control of the Disney Corporation, a period of expansion in Orlando ensued. Disney built up its property, installing more hotels, restaurants, and resorts until all areas adjoining the parks were filled with commercial services. Yet a segment of land across from the major highway in the area remained. Because of this highway, developing theme parks in the area was not practical. Eisner revisited Disney's idea of building a town on the property (EPCOT) and decided that this was the most advantageous use of the land.

Yet selling homes on Disney property would allow the residents of those homes a vote in the Reedy Creek Improvement District. Therefore, the company de-annexed the land before building began, selling it off to themselves in the form of a property management company. Disney was able to present this as a boon to Osceola County; by de-annexing the land, Disney was offering up the prospect of homeowners who would pay taxes to the county government. Thus, Celebration appears to have provided a happy compromise between Disney and local government: Disney keeps exclusive control over its universe, and local government gets a boost in its tax base.

But it is not clear that Celebration actually has been a boon for Osceola County. For example, the Celebration School was built before there was demand for a school, thereby robbing precious resources from other schools in the area badly in need of infrastructural improvements (Burstein 1995). Although Disney contributed a remarkable nine million dollars to Celebration's teaching academy, the school still cost the district another ten million dollars—a significant outlay for a school that was not yet needed while other schools in the district suffered from overcrowding and crumbling facilities!

The school serves as a friction point between Disney and the rest of Osceola County because the school board is the one external governing body that Disney could not eliminate from Celebration. Florida state law regulates that all public schools must be overseen by an elected local school board. In order to receive necessary monies for the Celebration School, Disney began pouring money into the campaign coffers of school board candidates (Burstein 1995). Before Celebration was conceived, Disney did not have an effect on local school politics; now it has become the largest financial interest behind it. Some observers would point to the teaching academy attached to Celebration and argue that the entire district must benefit from the pedagogical innovations that emerge from the academy. And to some extent, they would be correct—although teachers from all over the country come to seminars at Celebration School. But Disney also has reserved exclusive marketing rights over the educational materials developed at the academy. The system is ingenious: in exchange for subsidizing the academy and teacher visits to it, Disney is able to profit from the materials that are distributed from the academy to teachers across the country. (All of the teachers who come to the academy are unquestionably exposed to the advantages of Disney's educational materials.) Although this may seem like an ideal example of mutual benefit, the Osceola County School Board now must contend with issues of marketing and profit-making in order to maintain its district. The teaching center swallows many of the districts resources; it must be successful in order for the district to recoup their expenditures. Thus, Disney has been able to convert the local school board into an inadvertent partner for the Disney Corporation.

The hospital has also been a mixed blessing. In fact, Celebration Health was not able to obtain the necessary license for inpatient services because of the well-documented surplus of hospital beds in the area. Local hospitals had an occupancy rate of 44 percent the year before Celebration Health built their enormous inpatient wing (Mycek 1998). Disney's facility only adds to the glut of health care availability in the area, making the economic viability of other hospitals more precarious.

Celebration's exclusive management is not incorporated into local government. For now, Disney retains control over its development. All services are privatized. This state of affairs, however, is a temporary matter. Disney officials are quick to point out that once the development is complete, after a short transitional period, residents of Celebration will be able to elect their own Homeowners Association. However, a careful reading of the regulations that every homeowner must sign indicates that the association will have to ask permission to change any of the regulations that the Disney Corporation has established. Furthermore, a majority of landowners may override any decision that the association will make. Although this may seem like a provision for local owners to maintain control over their elected association, Disney will always be the majority landowner in Celebration, because it has set aside half of the property to be preserved "for environmental reasons." Thus, Celebration will never be a democracy.

But perhaps this is precisely what makes it a community. Certainly Celebration residents associate security with community, in a fashion remarkably reminiscent of Sennett's description of adolescence. But while Sennett argues that community is about the security that comes from purity, I would argue that Celebration indicates that what is comforting about community is relinquishing control. Certainly the principal designer of Celebration, Robert Stern, has come to see community as a social condition that requires giving up personal freedom. Invoking the authority of Tocqueville, Stern claims that Celebration is really the model of democratic freedom: "In a freewheeling capitalist society, you need controls—you can't have community without them. It's right there in Tocqueville; in the absence of an aristocratic hierarchy, you need firm rules to maintain decorum. I'm convinced these controls are actually liberating to people. It makes them feel their investment is safe. Regimentation can release you" (Pollan 1997, 80). One can assume that Stern is referring to Tocqueville's observations about democratic mores replacing the formal caste system of aristocracy. However, a glance at Tocqueville's discussion of democratic despotism reveals that such informal forms of control can degenerate toward mindless conformism as well. Tocqueville refuses to label the form of oppression located in democracies as tyranny; instead he tries to describe the process by which human self-determination is gently prodded away from citizens:

> That power is absolute, thoughtful of detail, orderly, provident, and gentle. It would resemble paternal authority if, fatherlike, it tried to prepare its charges for a man's life, but on the contrary, it only tries to keep them in perpetual childhood. It likes to see the citizens enjoy themselves, provided that they think of nothing but enjoyment. It gladly works for their happiness but wants to be the sole agent and judge thereof. It provides for their security, foresees and supplies their necessities, facilitates their pleasures, manages their principal concerns, directs their industry, makes rules for their testaments, and divides their inheritances. Why should it not entirely relieve them from the trouble of thinking and all the cares of living? (Tocqueville 1969, 667)

It would be difficult to find a more apt description of the authority that governs the residents of Celebration.

But it is crucial to remember that people chose this form of authority for themselves. As Stern points out, "This isn't some sort of gulag. It's a place you *want* to live in. And to live in a community, you have to give up some of your freedoms. You cannot pile all of your automobiles in the front yard. This is what being in a community is" (Rymer 1996). Stern presents living in a community as a necessary sacrifice of freedom; interviews with residents seem to indicate that it is precisely the sacrifice of freedom that attracts them to Celebration. For instance, what is unusual about Celebration is not the presence of covenant controls that are designed to keep up property values, but the breadth of them. In fact, Disney has even made it a breach of the covenant to have any window coverings that are not white or off-white. A couple that put in a door with beveled glass that did not match the prescribed pattern book received a stern letter from the manager of Celebration, as did a woman who put up red curtains (Franzt 1998). This is a truly remarkable intrusion into the realm of personal choice on the part of the Celebration covenant. Yet, unlike what most people say about Americans, personal choice does not appear to be what these residents most value. In fact, residents seem to embrace these regulations as a sort of guarantee that Celebration will remain the kind of place they want to live. Residents make claims like "with Disney, I have total confidence" and "I'm happy Disney will retain control for the next twenty years or so if it means the quality will remain high" (Kroloff 1997). In this case, brand recognition helps to ensure the myth of community.

I would argue that the search for community is not as much about adolescence as it is about childhood—more specifically, idealized childhood. And this is why it seems dreadfully important that Celebration is deliberately evocative of one's mythical childhood. Celebration offers the idea of total control and the elimination of chance and insecurity. Russ Rymer reported that the original marketing video for Celebration at the real estate office (one shown before the houses were built, which therefore could interview no residents) used the pleasures of childhood as its main pitch. "There is a place that takes you back to that time of innocence, a place where the biggest decision is whether to play kick the can or king of the hill. A place of caramel apples and cotton candy, secret forts and hopscotch in the streets. That place is here again, in a new town called Celebration" Rymer 1996, 68). Note the deliberate ambiguity of this message. Celebration may aim to give residents' children the idealized innocent experience, but the pitch actually makes it seem like adults will be able to recapture this magical frame of mind as well. Although adults may not be able to recapture the lost faith of childhood, they will at least be comforted to know that someone else is in charge in Celebration. Consider the negotiation between wanting self-determination and relishing external control in this statement by a Celebration resident: "Everyone's input is welcome. Disney's doing an excellent job of staying in the background. Behind the scenes they are doing a lot, and while they have to control things, I think they really want to step back" (Pollan 1997).

Readily apparent is a general confusion about what democracy is, as well as distaste for politics itself. Government is associated with discord, disharmony, unpleasantness. In contrast, community is about agreement, harmony, and friendship. One Celebration resident observed, "This community is made up of people with some pretty basic agreements about wanting to try new things, take some risks, wanting to be at the beginning of something. This transcends politics. We are big liberals, but our best friends in town are total conservatives. We share fundamental beliefs about doing what is important for the community and families" (Kroloff 1997). Because politics is viewed as an unpleasant task, it seems no sacrifice at all to relinquish self-government in exchange for a "responsive community." Celebration residents often use the term "responsive" to describe Disney's administration of the town, an interesting conjunction with the language of communitarianism. One Celebration resident proclaimed, "It is definitely a democracy, because we can go to town hall and express our feelings. It's a very responsive government" (Pollan 1997).

Celebration illustrates that Americans still value freedom. But this version of freedom means liberation both from insecurity and from responsibility, which also means from freedom from choice. In this sense, then, community really is the opposite of the marketplace and of the bureaucratic state that continues to offer a host of admittedly often undesirable choices. The irony of consumer capitalism is that it now offers a product, community, which portends to relieve the burden of choices faced by citizens of a consumer culture.

The meaning of community as relinquishing choice has been heralded in recent communitarian literature quite clearly. In Alan Ehrenhalt's book *The Lost City: The Forgotten Virtues of Community in America,* the author observes: "To worship community and choice together is to misunderstand what community is all about. Community means not subjecting every action in life to the burden of choice, but rather accepting the familiar and reaping the psychological benefits of having one less calculation to make in the course of the day" (Ehrenhalt 1995, 23). And indeed, why should we be concerned that people give up the right to colored curtains in their houses, follow a pattern book to decide which shrubs to plant in their yards, or don't want their neighbors to be allowed to park pick-up trucks on their street?

Tocqueville suggests the reason why the comforts of "community" should be regarded with suspicion. "It really is difficult to imagine how people who have entirely given up managing their own affairs could make a wise choice of those who are to do that for them" (Tocqueville 1969, 669). The lull of stability and being taken care of in smaller areas, such as home decor, easily slide toward larger questions such as educational policies, zoning decisions, and choosing representatives for government. During the 1960s, "community" was often used as a signal of collective self-determination. Today "community" often indicates collective disengagement.

In the end, what makes Celebration unique is Disney's involvement. Disney has long been associated with the production of fantasy, and in its theme parks demonstrates an almost seamless ability to manipulate reality on a grand scale. Additionally, the word "Disney" is almost synonymous with childhood due to fifty years of dominating children's entertainment. This reputation makes people more readily acquiesce in relinquishing control over their lives to Disney, but is exactly why others resist the idea of Disney's involvement in town planning. Disney's involvement and control makes it possible to have the fantasy of community, of control by someone else—total security—almost come true. What is instructive and sobering about Celebration is that it shows exactly how far people are willing to go to indulge their fantasies.

Celebration is being hailed as a model for future development in this country and even around the world. Another prominent developer expressed hope that now that the prototype had been built, with the help of computers other towns like Celebration will be built much more quickly. Charles Fraser, of Hilton Head, calculates that with the forecasted population growth in the United States being 80 million people over the next thirty years, many new places to live will have to be developed. He states, "We need three to four thousand Celebrations just to scratch the surface of their needs" (*Economist* 1995). But Celebration is not terribly different from other developments in this country known as "gated communities," except in the fact that it does not have a guarded gate around it to provide increased "security." Homeowners regularly give up the rights of self-government when they sign their mortgages under covenant restrictions, and they also acquiesce to invasions of privacy and reduction of personal choice in the interest of maintaining property values or "financial security." Celebration and developments like it appeal to an enormous number of people in this country (Kohn 2004).

For centuries, the bourgeois used their wealth to buy visions of their own powers—after all, "a man's home is his castle." It is ironic that at the beginning of this millennium, those who have money want to buy a fantasy of someone else being in charge of their lives. Celebration demonstrates how we can stimulate our desire for community, yet simultaneously avoid it. The signals of small-town living (front porches, flags, and girls on bikes) coexist comfortably in a suburb that actually promotes little interaction. Consumer capitalism gives us our desired community without the drawbacks of actually living in one. But it is not possible to separate the fantasy of community from its actuality so neatly. Part of the desire for community includes a wish for someone else to be in control. Providing for the dream may require that consumers relinquish their self-determination. The ease with which Disney has sold home buyers on the promise of an antidemocratic social organization is troubling. If community is defined as a place without discord, without politics, without cost, this is a dangerous myth indeed. The fantasy of permanent childhood may ultimately lead to its realization. It is clear that we will have to look away from our imaginary past for an alternative to capitalist individualism.

6

UTOPIAN VISION AS COMMODITY FETISH

Social Imagineering in Postmodern Capitalism

> Criticism has plucked the imaginary flowers from the chain, not in order that man shall bear the chain without caprice or consolation but so that he shall cast off the chain and pluck the living flower.
>
> —KARL MARX, *The Early Writings*

The tradition established by Tönnies in *Community and Society* remains the dominant mode of interpreting community. As this tradition would have it, society is alienating, individualistic, bureaucratic, impersonal, economic, and political. Community, in contrast, is none of these things. As I have established in this book, this idea still maintains a remarkable hold over most theories of community. For that reason, community, when employed as the central tool of social theorizing, occludes economic and political issues, while at the same time importing a natural or noncoercive view of sociality. It is no wonder that community seems to be the answer to all that ails us.

Using community as the nodal point of social theory has in part avoided the problems of contemporary society, not solved them. Hence I believe that it is crucial to overcome this intellectual tradition: community cannot be seen as the opposite of society, but rather as a dream that society has concocted for itself. Community is also understood quite frequently as a form of nostalgia, but this analysis has provided ample evidence to the contrary. Communities are sometimes, but certainly not always, evocative of the past, mythical or not. Community also holds the promise of an alternative future, as the work of the many feminists included here demonstrates.

If community is neither a utopian "other" nor a reminiscence, what is it today? How can we explain its nearly universal appeal and our common longing? It seems to me the answer lies is the *Gesellschaft* side of the equation, which for too long has been ignored, rather than viewed in relation to its created opposite, *Gemeinschaft*.

There are several dynamics that seem unique. First, when taken out of the context of theory, community is either in the past or the future, but never in the present. When we move to actualize it, it seems to disappear through our fingertips—what we thought might be community evaporates—but the desire, curiously, remains. It is tempting to account for this dynamic by pointing to the inevitable gap between ideal and real. While all ideas are only imperfectly realized, very few have the universal appeal of community. It is remarkable that so many people have this ideal without having consciously developed or elaborated it. So community is not an idea or theory as much as a ghostly apparition that haunts us. Most people do not study community, so how is it that so many have such a strong sense of what it might be? Because community is not an idea on the order of, say, the social contract or democracy, we cannot treat it as merely another slip between theory and praxis.

However, theories of consumerism provide insight into idealized communities and our processes of producing these ideals and consuming them. This is not to say that community exists only as a commodity, though the discussion of Celebration suggests that at times it can become one. Not all communities have been commodified, but ironically enough, the ones that have are generally not recognized as *communities* as we idealize them. The interaction between our *vision* of community and the world that seems to lack it is most aptly characterized by the processes of commodity fetishism. I believe this demonstrates how thoroughly modes of consumption have come to influence our relationship to the world and our possibilities within it. Actualization has come to be familiar as conquest of a specific object outside of ourselves, and defining ourselves is most easily accomplished through a collection of goods and services. Chain stores and catalogs create bonds of objects, as households around the country and even the world are filled with identical objects. You may spot your children's clothes on others at the park, and sleep on sheets identical to ones in your friends' guest room.

Before I can assert exactly how I believe ideas of community are influenced by consumer capitalism, it is prudent to establish what I am *not* arguing. By describing a materialist dimension to theories of community, I do not wish to endorse economic reductionism. Our dreams of perfect togetherness are not products of advertising executives. These are not mirages designed specifically to keep our noses to the grindstone and wallets open. Although one result of these ideals and how they function is to support current economic processes, they were not created with the exclusive intention of doing so. This would be known as the manipulationist version of consumer behavior, a theory that claims that our desires are implanted in us from outside influences (Campbell 2000; Packard 2000; Schudson 1986). Not only does this theory suggest a conspiracy of a sort unprecedented in history, it also assumes that humans are entirely malleable and are uninterested in creating desires or capable of carrying proclivities for certain feelings or objects.

Nor am I charging, like John Freie in his book *Counterfeit Community: The Exploitation of Our Longing for Connectedness* (1998), that we are fooled into accepting marketing facsimiles of community instead of the real thing. Once again, I think this seriously underestimates the agency of consumers as well as their savvy. What even casual observation of consumer behavior rapidly reveals is that consumers do not have their desires met, but they continue to buy anyway. Hence, the satisfaction of desire is not the ultimate goal. Desire itself is what propels the imagination, not its consummation. Freie misses this aspect of consumer behavior in his work. Furthermore, he implies that there is a "real" community that can be distinguished from its counterfeit counterpart. Very often our dreams of community seem more real than the communities we experience. Our desires and emotions *are* real, though, and are formed in a concrete political, social, and economic context. Who is to say that our ideal communities are counterfeit rather than an integral part of the reality that creates them?

There has been some work among economists responding to poststructuralist theories of identity constitution. These thinkers have tried to merge economic theory with social and cultural theories to provide a more integrated look at identity in capitalist societies. Jack Amariglio and Antonio Callari's work is a recent installment in the tradition of Lukacs and Benjamin, which sees commodity fetishism as both an economic and a social phenomenon. Amariglio and Callari emphasize commodity fetishism's role in subject constitution—not as a determining agent, but rather as a discursive element in the process. "Premised on a nondeterminist approach our rendition of commodity fetishism depicts the social constitution of the individual as a 'precondition' for commodity trade as much as an effect of this trade" (Amariglio and Callari 1993, 190). To restate the problem: Do we become who we are through consumption, or do we consume because of who we are? The similarity with the dilemma of relating the individual and membership in the community is immediately apparent: Do we become who we are through membership in communities, or do we join particular communities because of who we are? In both cases the answer is more complicated than the polarized options offered. In keeping with theories of subject constitution we can see subjectivity as a continuously evolving process, in which both commodity fetishism and community membership play a role. This chapter explicitly links these two phenomena in yet another fashion: How do we as consumers see communities and our membership in them, and how does commodity fetishism affect the kinds (or even existence) of communities available to us? In other words, how does capitalism affect political imagination today?

CONSUMER DESIRE AND IMAGINEERING COMMUNITY

Colin Campbell's book *The Romantic Ethic and the Spirit of Modern Consumerism* presents a persuasive description of modern consumerism. Campbell begins by identifying the unique aspects of modern desire and the consumption patterns that it creates. The central puzzle is why and how consumers today generate a seemingly endless desire for objects. Campbell distinguishes between traditional and modern hedonism, suggesting that traditional hedonism was attached to specific sensation, while the modern variety is based upon emotions more generally. Campbell traces the historical evolution of hedonism from one form into the other, a process he dates to the Enlightenment. "A natural consequence of this fundamental shift in world-view was that emotions were relocated 'within' individuals, as states which emanated from some internal source, and although these were not always 'spiritualized,' there is a sense in which the disenchantment of the external world required as a parallel process some 'enchantment' of the psychic inner world" (Campbell 1987, 73). This shift creates a new form of hedonism, one that is limited only by the scope of one's imagination rather than the extent of one's sensual experience. Imagination provokes emotions, including pleasure. Hence we can imagine our hearts' desires, and experience pleasure while doing so. Individuals can thereby exercise total control over their imaginations and pleasures, without the assistance of any outside stimuli. Campbell declares, "This is the distinctively modern faculty, the ability to create an illusion which is known to be false but felt to be true" (78).

This observation helps to explain why so many have such a strong sense of what community should, would, or could feel like, at the same time that most would deny having any such experience. Significantly, it also makes clear the paradoxical pleasure at work here—we are free to experience the joy and warmth of community, but only within our own minds.

Campbell also points out that modern, imaginative hedonism means that desire itself provides pleasure, which is interrupted only by the process of gratification. *Wanting* rather than *having* becomes the focus of consumer experience, illuminating why consumers so quickly shift their desires to another object once a previous focus has been gratified. The desire itself pleases us and can be infinitely replenished if we just refocus our imaginations away from what we have to what we *might* have.

The emphasis upon wanting rather than having captures the dynamics present in our visions and experiences of community. Visions of sociality pervade consumer images—families, small towns, friendly neighbors. The model of consumption allows us to desire these images or find them pleasurable at the same time that we might, for example, flee family gatherings in tears, find small towns provincial, or be bothered by nosy neighbors. Perhaps because community has been defined as the opposite of what we have (society), it is especially attractive as a collection of emotions and images attached to different consumer goods. Community and consumerism move together, mutually reinforcing systems of desire and wanting, complemented by never having or achieving. Community is the opposite of what we have, and hence eternally desirable as the unknown. Consumption teaches us to desire, never expecting gratification; thereby community as an ideal becomes especially conducive to commodification.

Campbell points out two phenomena that result from modern consumerist behavior. First, modern, imaginative hedonism causes a withdrawal from the physical world, as inner worlds can provide so much more internal pleasure. Second, consumer desire "also generates that dissatisfaction with reality which facilitates imaginative speculation about the gratification novel products might bring" (95). Viewing these two tendencies conjunctionally, Campbell's conception of modern, imaginative hedonism helps explain why visions of community provide us with a sense of dissatisfaction with the world as it exists, hence hinting at the possibility of social critique and change, while at the same time drawing us away from the commitment to changing the world necessary to achieving that vision.

More than any other single explanation, the model of consumerism suggests an exceedingly complicated relationship between our desire for community and our desire to achieve it. It can account for our pervasive desire for community and our simultaneous denial of having experienced it. The pleasure inherent in the desire of wanting something other than what one has explains why ideals of community offer the promise of critique at the same time that they strangely satiate those that dream them. Consumptive desire allows us to act according to our desire for community, yet never especially want or expect that desire to be gratified. Instead, the mirage of community continually works to draw us into the future or daydream into a mythical past—it is a repository of our desires for another life, but without the danger to the status quo that such social dissatisfaction might provide.

COMMUNITY AS A COMMODITY

Since contemporary visions of community are shaped by the same processes that fuse consumptive desire, we need to analyze how community exists as a commodity. The last chapter provided a stark example of community and its commodification: Disney markets community, and people buy it. Now it is time to explore the more subtle ramifications of the commodification of community. Despite the easy proliferation of images of community in marketing, consumer capitalism and sociality are not as easily reconciled as it may appear. I have already pointed out the paradox of consumptive imagination at work: we live in our dream communities in our own minds, with no necessary participation on the part of others. This is only the first irony in the existence of the community/commodity relation.

If ideals of community can exist as commodities, this is one indication of how dominant modes of consumerism have become in our society. Guy Debord's *The Society of the Spectacle* (1994) is one of the most provocative reading of the character of society in late (one might even say post-) capitalism. Debord's work is informed by Georg Lukacs's theory of commodity fetishism (1988). These two theorists represent a strain of Marxist thought that emphasizes the social ramifications of commodification. Lukacs distinguishes modern capitalism from earlier economic forms through the universalization of the commodity. In order that even laborers will see their own efforts as a commodity for exchange—in short, for labor to become alienated—commodification must become universal. "To achieve that it would be necessary . . . for the commodity structure to penetrate society in all its aspects and to remould it in its own image" (Lukacs 1988, 85). Naturally, this remolding of society in the image of the commodity would include our ideas of sociality.

Debord begins with Lukacs's observations and attempts to describe exactly how society has been shaped by commodity fetishism in *The Society of the Spectacle*. He begins his text with a quote from Feuerbach: "But certainly for the present age, which prefers the sign to the thing signified, the copy to the original, representation to reality, the appearance to the essence . . . illusion only is sacred, truth profane. Nay, sacredness is held to be enhanced in proportion as truth decreases and illusion increases, so that the highest degree of illusion comes to be the highest degree of sacredness" (Debord 1994, 11). While Feuerbach wrote of religion, today what Debord calls "the spectacle" has become the central, and sacred, illusion that binds society.

The crucial point here is that Debord's theory of the spectacle meditates upon what a society entirely subsumed to the logic of commodity fetishism would look like. I believe idealizations of community provide one particularly salient example of how our ideals and imaginations can become subverted by material conditions. What happens when utopian vision becomes commodity fetishism? The spectacle acts as a divider—not just a screen, but something that creates alienation.

> The spectacle divides the world into two parts, one of which is held up as self-representation to the world, and is superior to the world. The spectacle is simply the common language that bridges this division. Spectators are linked only by a one-way relationship to the very center that maintains their isolation from one another. The spectacle thus unites what is separate, but it unites it only *in its separateness*. (22)

This description of the one-way relationships that are substituted for reciprocal ones illuminates how we become separated by our commodity/community. Ironically, we share a vision, an image of sociality that further alienates us.

Consumer desire is never satisfied, as Campbell so clearly points out, but here consumer desire makes its object eternally unachievable for other reasons as well. As consumers we are driven to work progressively longer hours in order to achieve the incomes that will support our desires, keeping us away from our families, neighbors, churches, and other groups. This is one layer of difficulty that must be overcome in order to engage in community building. A second layer of consumer consciousness hinders our community development as well. When we relate to community as we do to any other commodity, as a desirable object or feeling that exists outside of ourselves, we relieve ourselves of responsibility for it, making it an entirely impossible goal. Our way of envisioning community as something to be desired and imagined halts the impetus to build actual communities. The communities we live in are devalued and disregarded in favor of superior, imagined representations.

This is exactly why Giorgio Agamben's theory of the coming community that will be birthed via consumer capitalism is so problematic. Agamben proclaims that through the proliferation of representation in advertising, we have come to the consciousness that there is no necessary referent between sign and signifier. Once the assumed transparency between what we appear to be and what we are breaks down, we become free to relate to one another and find ourselves. The clear distinction between representation and existence provides a scrim behind which life can flourish. Agamben claims, "And yet the process of technologization, instead of materially investing the body, was aimed at the construction of a separate sphere that had practically no point of contact with it: What was technologized was not the body but its image. This, the glorious body of advertising, has become the mask behind which the fragile, slight human body continues its precarious existence" (Agamben 1993, 49). Consumer capitalism has given birth to a new community, revealed by the inability of commodities to maintain their fetishism. Agamben's community becomes a wedge of isolation as well as the opiate for this social alienation. Agamben believes, thirty years after Debord published *The Society of the Spectacle*, that the spectacle has become so apparent to all of us that it can be peeled away like a mask, and can protect a rejuvenated sociality. This seems entirely too optimistic, for as Campbell aptly points out, the modern, hedonistic imagination gains pleasure even from images that it *knows* to be false. Knowledge that our images of community are false is not enough to liberate us from their ill effects or subvert the pleasure we derive from them.

It is important to emphasize that Debord's "spectacle" is not the same as Baudrillard's "simulations." Baudrillard claims that image and referent are equally counterfeit. "Disneyland is presented as imaginary in order to make us believe the rest is real, when in fact all of Los Angeles and the America surrounding it are no longer real, but of the order of the hyper-real and of simulation" (Baudrillard 1983, 25). This observation is based upon Baudrillard's critique of Marx (1975), whereby Baudrillard claimed that there is no longer any relationship between use value and value. By severing the relationship between base and superstructure, Baudrillard detaches the images that circulate between us from social relations.

Debord's theory of the spectacle maintains the linkage between social images and the economic relations that they mediate. It is not that community as a commodity is a set of images detached from all social relations—instead the commodity that is community becomes the mediator of social relations. The spectacle relates to the conditions that it obscures—it is not a free-floating signifier. In fact, one might argue that Baudrillard's theory of image is part of the spectacle itself. "Understood on its own terms, the spectacle proclaims the predominance of appearances and asserts that all human life, which is to say all social life, is mere appearance" (Debord 1994, 13). The spectacle denies any reality outside of itself, hence becoming the primary form of social mediation. When Agamben and Baudrillard detach our fantasies and representations from "reality," the oppositional nature of these visions is lost.

We hope that our ideals can serve as a reference point when they conflict with real conditions. Ideals should define what has gone awry in the world, and provide some lead in how we might overcome the gap between material world and ideal. When utopian vision functions as a commodity, it obscures the real rather than serving as a critique of it. Furthermore, the interplay between ideal and material world does not result in a productive tension, where practice will inform theory and theory will help define what actions might need to be taken. As our desires for community are located in one object after another, the interplay between ideal and material becomes like an endless feedback loop—leading to change in neither. Instead of using our ideals and our disappointment therein to drive us to change the world, we can simply move onto another consumer experience to have our vision titillated once more. This also gives some sense of why the ideal of community remains remarkably constant even in the face of an ever-changing world: there is no dynamic tension between the desire and its gratification, only an endless cycle of desire and partial fulfillment.

I believe this is the greatest challenge facing those who imagine different, better worlds today. How can we recapture the collective imagination and make it demand concrete satisfaction instead of being satisfied by desire? Is desiring human sociality enough to establish ourselves as sentient creatures? The task of the theorist is to problematize and to reveal the relationship between ideal and material, making sure that our dreams of community are not substituting or even killing attempts to construct it.

I do not intend that this discussion should provoke despair or scorn for the oppositional possibilities in community. My theory of the community/commodity explicitly links our utopian ideals and current political, economic, and ideological formations. I do so in order to propose that achieving our ideals will take radical action and a more complete social overhaul than most proponents of community would comfortably endorse. Above all, I am optimistic that so many of us still sense and dream that there is a different and better way to live. "Every epoch, in fact, not only dreams the one to follow but, in dreaming, precipitates its awakening" (Benjamin 1999, 13). Current social, economic, and political realities have obscured the abilities of our imaginations to lead us to a different way of living. We must change the world in order to free our dreams.

7

COMMUNITY IN PRACTICE

How is a community built? What are the ingredients that seem to make it work? While much of the discussion thus far has been about how we imagine communities, it is important to conclude with some observations about how imagination becomes manifest in building and living in communities as well. The study of Celebration, Florida, gave an example of imagineering at work with a blank canvas; comparing this new urbanist construct and the transformation of a classical suburban development in West Philadelphia provides some surprising insights. Although the two neighborhoods are different in many ways, there are instructive similarities between the new development and the neighborhood that is now over a century old. In both cases, a large institution or corporation has driven the development of the neighborhood, funded it, and self-consciously chosen to develop according to the ideals of community that I have discussed. Families, public participation, inclusiveness, and specific values are stressed in both areas, and residents talk about identity and belonging as a central reason for living where they do. Interestingly, the neighborhoods have also studied one another. West Philadelphia has long been a mecca for architecture, both residential and otherwise. Grand homes with prominent front porches and welcomingly sized streets and house fronts have helped to inspire the design of new urbanist developments such as Celebration. Conversely, when community members in West Philadelphia convened to investigate building a new school, they looked at Celebration School for the newest ideas about community-friendly educational institutions.

West Philadelphia's revival was by and large funded by the University of Pennsylvania, which is located on one edge of the neighborhood. As I discussed in Chapter 5, the Disney Corporation underwrote the development of Celebration. Without large institutional sponsorship, it seems difficult for communities to survive, as is evident in company towns throughout the country that falter when their economic bases disappear. Communities rarely have the internal funds available to take on either large-scale redevelopment or first-time development. Real estate developers help to stabilize neighborhoods, but they don't have the ability to, for example, build a downtown before the neighborhood exists, as Disney did in Celebration. Nor will smaller businesses likely provide for extra trash pick up or security patrols, or underwrite mortgages and buy out delinquent land owners as the University of Pennsylvania did in West Philadelphia.

As most corporations are structured to meet quarterly profit reports where short-term rather than long-term investments and profits seem to drive decisions, capitalism alone cannot drive the kind of significant investment in community that was demonstrated by the Disney Corporation and the University of Pennsylvania. This shows that only very powerful institutional interests who have a vision beyond immediate profit (but who may well profit from their investment in community ultimately) will be able to engage in such an enterprise. On the other hand, this is also an argument for increasing the state's role in community development, since it is supposed to have the larger interests of the population in mind. Unfortunately, as it stands, as most businesses would be unable or unwilling to invest in such projects, and government is constrained through budget crises and a reduction of its vision and mission. With these two avenues missing, such community development projects, no matter how successful or even profitable, are bound to be rare.

The Disney Corporation and the University of Pennsylvania are each the largest employer in the respective regions of study. Both are able to wrestle special concessions from local governments, obtain special exemptions, and win the support of often recalcitrant local and state governments. In both cases, this economic pull has proved to be instrumental in the development and redevelopment of these communities. Yet one could argue that their identities as such very large players belie the ideal of community as a grassroots effort. If large corporate or institutional sponsorship is needed to navigate local ordinances, this demonstrates the inherent difficulties of creating community-based spaces today.

Aside from this parallel between the two projects, there are several others. In both neighborhoods, the public school has become the centerpiece of community development, an interesting fact considering the decline of support for public education in communities all over the United States. One might argue that the general decline of public schools makes those developments that invest in it all the more alluring. But I believe a more optimistic assessment is plausible. A good school can act as the heart of a community, generating increased emotional and physical investment in a neighborhood and serving as place where families come together to collectively participate and solve problems. Educational reform has led more educators and community leaders to see education as integrally connected to the communities around them, as evidenced by the development of service learning and community-based educational programs that are expanding at every level in the United States. Education can provide a crucial point of intersection for a community at large.

Likewise, both neighborhoods also have a diversity of housing options available, ranging from high- to low-priced homes, and also make available some rental properties. The income range extends far lower in the case of West Philadelphia, with single rooms renting for $300 per month, and apartments available starting at $400 per month. Increasing economic segregation marks the contemporary geography of the United States, thus the attempt to achieve income diversity is noteworthy.

Similarly, both neighborhoods attract new residents who specifically chose the area because of its community. Like residents in Celebration, West Philadelphians are self-consciously proud of their activism and community investment. Some residents have turned down job offers elsewhere because, as one person commented, "I've never seen a community like this anywhere else, and I refuse to give it up."

There are, however, crucial differences between West Philadelphia and Celebration. West Philadelphia has a tremendous diversity of racial and ethnic backgrounds. There are more than one hundred different countries of origin represented at the local elementary school. Despite rising housing prices, the neighborhood remains a destination for recent Vietnamese, Laotian, Indian, and West African immigrants. The neighborhood is also weighted by more than fifty years of economic depression; many of the houses, which are over a hundred years old, are literally collapsing from disrepair. Crime is still a problem, though the crime rate has significantly dropped in the past five years. Crime, trash, and blight make West Philadelphia a less desirable environment for many who can afford other options, yet make it affordable for those with fewer resources. Those with more resources move into the neighborhood as a choice: the more expensive houses have been restored and their prices are equivalent to the cost of living in a suburb. The wealthier residents have chosen this neighborhood over more solidly gentrified areas, and in large part cite the school and the community as their primary motivation for doing so. The median home price in West Philadelphia is $142,000, less than half the median home price in Celebration, now $300,000.

In the early 1990s West Philadelphia was most frequently in the news for neighborhood crime. The crack cocaine epidemic made it unsafe to walk through the neighborhood at any time of the day, and housing prices had fallen precipitously (the average price of homes was in the $50,000 range for a 2,600-square-foot home). Even long-term residents moved away, and the University of Pennsylvania was considering building a large wall to separate the campus from the neighborhood located to its west. Today housing prices have appreciated 300 percent in some areas, houses sell within days of being on the market, streets are crowded by strollers, homes are being refurbished on every block, and people are moving from New York City and commuting by train to work every day in order to live in the neighborhood. How did this turnaround happen? And what lessons can be learned about how ideals of community translate into practice? Finally, how did the market influence people's investment in and experience of community in this instance? The success of West Philadelphia provides a heartening model of inner-city renewal that is starting to be internationally recognized. Here is a piece of political imagination that has succeeded.

WEST PHILADELPHIA: HISTORY AND DESCRIPTION

The neighborhood under discussion was largely originally developed between 1890 and 1910, adjacent to the University of Pennsylvania, which moved to the west side of the Schuylkill river in 1871. New street car lines provided a ten-minute commute into the center of Philadelphia, making it possible to live in a spacious, luxurious house on a tree-lined street and yet work in the inner city. Most of the houses were built with servants' staircases and quarters. The houses are ornate and large (between 2,500 and 3,200 square feet), though on proportionately small plots. Interestingly, the neighborhood was one of the first of its kind, with exclusively residential streets and corridors of business concentrated into a few areas. Delores Hayden recently published an extensive study of suburban development in the United States. West Philadelphia falls into the general category of streetcar suburbs, early residential living areas that sprung up along streetcar lines in nineteenth-century cities. The area is relatively unique within this category, however. Hayden notes that most of these neighborhoods were working class, and "homes were usually on a modest scale" (Hayden 2003, 71). West Philadelphia, in contrast, was built for the management class and the housing is resplendent. In many ways, the neighborhood was the turn-of-the-century equivalent of contemporary developments that segregate residences and businesses. However, in the era before cars, the separation was much shorter and needed to be traversable by foot, though people relied upon the streetcars to take them into the heart of Philadelphia.

A local joke at the time was that the suburb was integrated, meaning it had both Protestants and Episcopalians. Ninety-seven percent of the population was white, although some large African American churches were built, indicating a small black population from the outset. Seventeen percent of the neighborhood residents were Irish, indicating the large servant population that lived with the wealthier families. Those in the register of the Philadelphia Society had addresses clustered in the downtown area. However, it was decided that addresses between Market and Pine Streets in the new neighborhood would also be colored "blue" and hence acceptable in polite society (Skaler 2002).

The Great Depression changed the fortunes of the still relatively new development. By 1946, crime, social problems, and blight had become systemic and rejuvenation efforts began through the foundation of a "Neighborhood Operations" society. Regional transportation was developed, and many families moved farther outside of the city, leaving much of the neighborhood to decay. Jewish immigrants took up residence on some streets and maintained the homes. Other sections were sold and subdivided, becoming low-income housing. In 1950 a smaller section of the neighborhood called Spruce Hill founded a community association, which would prove to be a formidable force through the present day. Despite efforts by such organizations, crime and blight continued to develop in the neighborhoods in West Philadelphia. The deindustrialization of the 1960s and 1970s hit the neighborhood hard, leaving the University of Pennsylvania the primary local employer.

The University of the Sciences and Drexel University are also located in the neighborhood today called University City. In the 1970s and 1980s the relationship between the neighborhood and the universities was extremely poor by all accounts. In 1987 the recession and crack epidemic that affected many inner-city neighborhoods led to a rapid decline in housing prices, an increase in crime, and even more "white flight" from the neighborhood. Crime skyrocketed, and the University of Pennsylvania discouraged students from living in or even walking into the neighborhood that bordered the campus. When crime worsened, eventually resulting in the deaths of some students and faculty, the University considered building a wall around the university to meet the concerns for safety among faculty, students, and staff.

However, in 1994, Judith Rodin, President of the University of Pennsylvania, decided that the University could no longer isolate itself from the problems of the surrounding communities. There were several high-profile murders in the University community that left parents and administrators outraged and demanding action. Faculty left the University after having unpleasant experiences in the community or being mugged on campus. The problem of faculty retention due to the immediate environment around the school was well documented and noted to those at the top of the University hierarchy.[1]

Pushed by crisis, the University of Pennsylvania decided to expand several existing programs in the mid 1990s. First, although the University had long had a community involvement office, they had few notable accomplishments upon which to build. In contrast, a program called the West Philadelphia Improvement Corps (WEPIC), which was developed out of an honors seminar at the University, had enjoyed the most long-standing success. Founded in 1985, the program was a school-based neighborhood revitalization program that involved faculty and students from the University of Pennsylvania, local school students, and the public school administration. In 1992, University of Pennsylvania professors Ira Harkavy and John Puckett published an article in *Planning for Higher Education* arguing that WEPIC could provide a model for all universities located near inner-city or rural areas suffering from poverty, crime, and community degeneration. They argued that becoming more involved in solving social problems would regenerate both universities and the communities near them. After conducting pilot programs for seven years, the authors argued, "[I] n a deteriorating inner community, the neighborhood school has the best chance of serving as the core institution for change, a new kind of community center that provides diverse services, serves as a gathering place, and galvanizes other community institutions, groups, and individuals. The school, its curriculum and its varied services, day and evening, becomes in effect the focal point of neighborhood activity, improvement and stabilization" (Harkavy and Puckett 2002, 31). They argued that universities and colleges are uniquely suited to support the effort to transform community schools, and that this change would benefit the University of Pennsylvania specifically by providing community research through "participatory action." It is this vision that continues to drive the depth and form of the University's commitment to the neighborhood.

1. In files in the University of Pennsylvania archives, I found multiple letters from different department and administrative chairs documenting when faculty members left or refused to come to the University because of concerns about safety.

The second important pilot project was an attempt on the part of local residents in the early 1990s to form a University City Development District based upon the model of the Center City Development District in downtown Philadelphia. The short-term project demonstrated that increased lighting and trash pick-ups could immediately improve the quality of life in the neighborhood (Lily 2004). However, state regulations prevented the levying of a special tax upon businesses in the neighborhood; therefore, the District died out as soon as the special funding, having been granted, was used up.

With pressure mounting from concerned parents, faculty leaving the university, applications dropping, and the crime rate increasing despite doubling campus security, the University of Pennsylvania was finally moved into action. University leaders decided upon three different approaches to stabilizing the neighborhood, reducing crime, and rescuing their real estate investments.

First, they revived and implemented the idea of a University City Development District, which began to provide an increased level of city services to the neighborhood to immediately improve safety. The University City Development District sponsors "ambassadors" who patrol the neighborhood on bike and foot from 11 AM until 3 AM every day. At any time there are fifteen to twenty ambassadors on the streets doing homeless outreach, giving directions, providing escorts, jump-starting cars, or helping in an emergency. The organization also has a maintenance staff that sweeps sidewalks and streets, removes graffiti and trash, cleans vacant lots, and tends street trees. Additionally, the University City Development District recruits businesses to the area, provides extra trash pick-up as the City's schedule does not allow it to maintain the neighborhood at a high standard, and pays for extra lighting. The organization stepped in to provide a basic standard of safety and cleanliness, which made the neighborhood more attractive to potential homeowners, current residents, students, and businesses. The University of Pennsylvania, Drexel University, and the University of the Sciences, along with voluntary contributions from other businesses and residents, fund the Development District.

Second, the University of Pennsylvania also extended a mortgage assistance plan that provided each university employee with $10,000 in assistance to buy a home in the designated neighborhood west of the campus. Previously the mortgages were only available for employees that earned less than $41,000 per year and were offered in Center City areas as well. The program was revised to target only the neighborhoods immediately adjoining the University and to include staff and faculty in the upper echelons of pay by lifting the salary cap. Recognizing that many of these large, old houses had fallen into disrepair, the University also provided up to $35,000 in loans for home repair, $7,000 of which was forgiven for every year the residents remained in the home. Within five years the entire loan would then be forgiven. A great impetus for University employees to move into the neighborhood was instigated, as this assistance would provide for an entire down payment and transfer tax in the depressed real-estate market. Having a virtually free house with money for repairs was enough to overcome many people's concerns about safety.

Finally, the University of Pennsylvania also developed plans for a kindergarten through eight-grade elementary school in the neighborhood as an extension of WEPIC. On a site owned by the University three blocks from campus was a private elementary school, the New School, that had long been assisted by the University. Forty percent of its students were children of faculty or staff at the University of Pennsylvania. The University decided, however, that it wanted to build a community-based school that would be accessible to all children in the neighborhood and thus cancelled the school's lease. This led to an uproar in the neighborhood, yet ultimately the University persisted in its vision. After the initial announcement was made, further community involvement and disagreement was brokered in the course of drawing the boundaries for the public school that was to replace the private one. The School of Education at the University of Pennsylvania helps to develop curriculum and serves as a resource for the new elementary school, called the Sadie Tanner Mosel Alexander Penn-Partnership School, and the University committed one thousand dollars of additional funding for every registered pupil for ten years to decrease class size and provide more resources. In return, the school also provides a place for educational research for the School of Education at the University. The public school is open to any child who lives within the designated boundaries, locally called the "catchment area."

While the elementary school is part of the Philadelphia public education system, the University of Pennsylvania still owns the property and maintains the grounds. Community leaders have indicated that this was one way to help ensure the University's continued commitment to the school. In return for helping fund the building of the school, the University of Pennsylvania wrestled many key concessions from the school district, including tempering the teachers' union's influence over staffing. (Staffing in Philadelphia public schools is generally assigned according to seniority. In order for the University to choose its own teachers for the school, the union had to agree to suspend the normal union regulations for this location.) In 2002 the building was designed according to the vision articulated by Harkavy and Puckett in 1992. It is located in the center of the neighborhood, has seminar rooms that can be used by the community and green areas that are open for public use after school, and is open at night for events such as exercise classes, basketball, free movies, and seminars on gardening and nutrition.

Many people credit the school as the key to the long-term stability of the neighborhood, as now families with small children compete to buy houses in the neighborhood. One local realtor commented, "If a house hasn't sold within a week in the Catchment area, something is seriously wrong with the price." The Penn-Partnership School provides one of the few excellent public educational alternatives at the elementary level in the city of Philadelphia. Home prices within the catchment area are frequently elevated by $80,000 to $100,000 in comparison to similar houses located just across the street, but that fall outside of the school's boundaries! It is also instructive to see how the presence of the school is rapidly changing the racial composition of the neighborhood. The upper grades of the school are almost entirely African American, while the lower grades are better integrated, evenly divided between international, Caucasian, and African-American students.

Today the neighborhood is both economically and racially diverse, as interspersed within the great homes are many apartment buildings, and many of the houses built for single families were subdivided in the subsequent seventy years of declining economic fortunes. Spruce Hill proper still has an owner occupancy rate of 18 percent, which is the lowest in the city, except for segments that are composed entirely of public housing. Studio apartments that rent for $400 per month are located on the same block as homes that now sell for $400,000.

While these three developments—the University City Development District, the mortgage assistance plan, and the reworking of the elementary school—helped the neighborhood recovery, a close analysis reveals that many factors must be in place for a community such as this one to thrive. In the following discussion, I will isolate these variables and present what I have come to see as the most important aspects in helping a community thrive.

ELEMENTS OF COMMUNITY PRACTICE

Leadership. As I observed in Chapter 4, frequently community is something that is envisioned as nonhierarchical in terms of race, gender, or economic status. This lack of hierarchy is considered crucial for participation. I argued that authority was a missing element in these theories. The results of interviewing dozens of people and observing community politics for years show that leadership is also a crucial aspect of community life that is all too often overlooked. Racial, gender, and economic hierarchies, among others, are so engrained in our society that conscious and deliberate leadership is needed to overcome them. Lack of hierarchy needs to be cultivated, it doesn't naturally occur. If organizations are going to include disparate groups, they need to work very hard to do so.

Second, with more demands on people's time than ever before, leaders need to inspire and channel effective community involvement. Too frequently leadership figures take on too many tasks themselves, instead of cultivating community by dispersing them. For instance, as I talked with one community leader she observed that even when her institution could afford to pay for repairs or special developments, she always chose to have affiliated persons collectively build, clean, or repair together at special events.

In West Philadelphia, there are multiple institutions that help to involve residents in the community, and the cooperative mentality seems to reproduce itself. There are cooperative bike repair spaces that provide bicycles for children who could not otherwise afford them, a cooperative food store and nursery school, and artistic groups such as the Spiral Q Puppet Theater, whose mission is to create community involvement and democratic participation through the arts. There are groups that support gardening efforts and the restoration of the public park, as well as a converted house that provides low-cost arts classes for residents. There are also co-housing units in the neighborhood, collectively owned coffee shops and businesses, and a venue for all-ages concerts that provides a space where teenagers from all over Philadelphia congregate. All of these organizations are in addition to the more standard structures of the local landscape: chambers of commerce, neighborhood organizations, PTAs, and churches. Although more chain stores are moving into the area in order to be near the University, many neighborhood businesses are still owner-operated. Many of them frequently donate services and goods to local institutions that engage in fund raising, ensuring strong loyalty.

Another example of leadership helping to foster community ties is the work of Barbara Klein, who founded St. Mary's Nursery School almost forty years ago. The school started as a playgroup, and has grown to become a daycare center that employs ten people and serves sixty children. Klein observed that parents felt more comfortable leaving their children in care where they knew there were other parents, so the school has always been run as a cooperative. Every day three or four different parents work in the classroom alongside paid staff. This means that parents get to know all the children, as well as one another as shifts often overlap. Parents help in the classroom, but as Klein observed, the idea of parent help was really for the sake of the parents. "They needed to get out, meet each other, and spend time with other kids besides their own. Once you see that all three-year-olds behave like that, you don't worry so much when your own child does it" (Klein 2004). Similarly, the school has three workdays a year when all parents come and collectively build needed amenities, cut trees, and clean the classrooms and playgrounds. Klein preferred to hire teachers from the immediate neighborhood, and now alumni of the nursery school are returning to work as teachers. This structure was a deliberate venture on the part of Klein. Community support, for both children and parents, is key to the health and happiness of families. Here, childcare is conceived as a support for families and community rather than as a replacement for them, and largely succeeds on these terms.

Structural Interdependence. In *City: Urbanism and Its End,* Douglas Rae observes that cities are relics from a particular era of American economic and political history (Rae 2003). Classical urbanism fit the needs of centralized manufacturing industries. With the development of regional transportation, neighborhoods such as this one in West Philadelphia offered the relatively wealthy nearby escapes from urbanism into more residential neighborhoods. With the development of alternating current electricity and affordable automobiles, the dream of residential living became democratized, as evidenced by the explosion of the less elaborate and more affordable suburbs that fanned like rings around American cities in the late 1940s and 1950s. Inner cities, and sometimes residential districts proximate to cities such as West Philadelphia, were abandoned, architectural relics of a time now past. Rae points out that cities are not as flexible as the society that spawned them. A society builds an infrastructure that meets its needs. Economies and populations are more flexible than built environments; therefore, as they change, the infrastructural environment of the city is no longer needed and falls into decay. Urban areas are the physical infrastructure of a centralized manufacturing economy whose time has passed, hence the crisis of urbanism in the late twentieth century. Cities cannot resurrect the economy and industries of the past, but are forced to reckon with the remnants of another era to make them best work in their own time. In the 1960s and 1970s urban redevelopment was embraced as the best answer, where old buildings were demolished and rebuilt from scratch. Today, however, the trend is to resurrect old neighborhoods and work with the elements of the past.

Rae believes that the era of cities as economic centers has ended, but other scholars such as Saskia Sassen believe that even a globalized, service-intensive economy creates a form of centralization in areas, which she calls global cities (1991). In the case of West Philadelphia the health and education industries have replaced manufacturing as the core of the region's economy. The University of Pennsylvania is now the city's largest employer, and the growing health-care industry is also overrepresented in the neighborhood. These institutions were present even during the neighborhood's decline during most of the twentieth century, so it is difficult to argue that their presence alone is responsible for the neighborhood's revival. Nonetheless, without the educational and health-care institutions located in the region, it is impossible to imagine that any urban renewal would have been possible.

Yet the infrastructure of the neighborhood plays a key role in maintaining and encouraging community spirit. Many of the houses are row homes, so they are literally attached to one another. More opulent houses are twins: large, ornate duplexes. A neighbor's front porch might start where another's ends, and houses frequently share gutters, drainpipes, walls, steps, and walks. While this kind of physical proximity does encourage interaction, it also provides a structural interdependence familiar to any resident in the neighborhood. If one resident's porch is leaking, the water drips onto her or his neighbor's porch as well. Neighbors commonly pool labor efforts and resources to fix problems with roofs, trees, foundations, and porches that affect multiple homes. Robert Frost may have observed that good fences make good neighbors. In this case, shared walls provide structural interdependence for neighbors. This structural interdependence draws in even those who would be less likely to become involved in the lives of others.

In addition to the conjoining of the private spaces of many homes, there are also many other shared spaces that create connections. There is a large public park in the neighborhood that hosts children's story times, public festivals, a farmers' market, chess tables, concerts, public movies, playgrounds, a soccer field for all ages, a basketball court, and sledding on snowy days. The park exists as the common ground for the entire neighborhood and is large enough that different groups can use it differently and simultaneously. As back yards do not have enough space for swing sets, or even sandboxes in many cases, children congregate at the park after school and every weekend.

Area businesses also work to create shared public space in the neighborhood. The owners of Abbraccio, an Italian restaurant, work to provide what they describe as a "third space." In their view, people need a third space different from their jobs and their homes where they can meet other people, and perhaps even feel comfortable entertaining others there as if it was their own space. The owners constructed a new building with a special dining room for families with young children, as well as a terrace and bar where there is live music and a happy hour. They also have special Sunday brunches, inviting residents to come and eat while hearing a presentation on a topic such as obtaining block grants, gardening in the city, or maintenance for old homes. Other businesses have included outdoor tables and terraces, even on busy streets, adding to the public traffic on the sidewalks that can create a connection between those inside and those on the sidewalk.

Time. Nothing can substitute for time clocked in a neighborhood, at a school, or on a block. The importance of time started to dawn upon me when I lived in a neighborhood in New Orleans. Neighbors would spend hours standing in the front yard talking about nothing in particular. In typical Yankee fashion, I wondered to myself why these people didn't have more to do! Today there are several octogenarians that live on my block. They sit on their front porches and report on any and all activity that happens in the course of the day. Kids are kept out of the street, neighbors are reminded to water flowers, and trash is picked up as soon as it blows up the street from the departing trash truck. The average American work week is now forty-eight hours, not including time for commuting. We can start to see immediately why community life is exceedingly hard to sustain no matter what a person's proclivities or desires. All of the most vibrant communities I have been a part of have a number of unemployed or underemployed individuals, whose time is less constrained and whose involvement may therefore be more pronounced.

This is one very concrete reason why it is important to have diversity amongst members of a community. If everyone in a neighborhood or group is pursuing a demanding, successful career, there will always be a shortage of volunteers who can accomplish tasks. On the other hand, people like retired folks, college students in between semesters, immigrant mothers just learning to speak English and looking for assistance to do so, and freelance photographers will all be more likely to have time to contribute to accomplish projects. This is why having a diverse price for housing is key to maintaining a community. If someone who works part time, is retired, or is a student or stay-at-home father could not afford to live in the area, then the army of volunteer labor would be severely curtailed.

The Spruce Hill Community Association in the West Philadelphia neighborhood I've been discussing builds upon the basic premise that working with neighbors is the way to improve quality of life. It has neighborhood block grants that anyone in the area can apply for. These can total up to $4,000 over a number of years for trees, garden pits, curb repair, or the redesign of row home fronts, for example. Every grant must have evidence of community involvement in the planning of the grant and in providing matching funds. Volunteer labor is counted as matching funds. Volunteer time is clocked at ten dollars per hour, so a group of ten individuals working for ten hours one weekend will contribute the labor that will match a grant of $1,000 from the association. These block grants have been remarkably successful in helping to create an improved environment. Trees and plants line all of the streets, and it is not uncommon to see groups of neighbors out on their selected work days breaking up concrete for space for new trees and flowers, or helping to build a new stone wall on their street. The Spruce Hill Community Association recently won a national award for urban gardening and greening efforts.

In such an environment, it is not hard to become involved, if one has the time. In the course of conducting interviews in West Philadelphia I was drafted to serve on another board and into three other community projects! One man told me that a few months after he moved into the neighborhood he was out trying to remove a rusty old sign on his block. His neighbor walked across the street and handed him a membership to the Spruce Hill Community Association because it looked like he had the right spirit.

Debate/Acrimony. Looking back over the past fifty years of history it is clear is that the West Philadelphia neighborhood has not always been a harmonious community. There have been and continue to be vehement and even hostile disagreements between different parties in the neighborhood. For many years, the division between university administrators and community residents was particularly sharp. Many residents banded together in fighting a common enemy, the University that was developing the neighborhood. Now the University has agreed not to develop any more sites in

Spruce Hill for their own use and is instead expanding to the East. While some leaders in the neighborhood consider the University their greatest ally, others are angry that the University does so much "for the neighborhood" instead of "with it."

For example, Larry Falcon, a local minister who works with school children, is one of the most vocal opponents of gentrification, the University City Development District, and now the designation of Spruce Hill as a Historical Site. He heads an organization called Neighbors Against McPenntrification. He attends all meetings where development plans are discussed and has even brought lawsuits against the University. Reverend Falcon has also been instrumental in other neighborhood pursuits, including helping to develop a program to fight crime and drugs with community members, SOMAD (South of Market Against Drugs).

Falcon argues that the University determined that its more limited fortress vision was never going to work to make the campus safe. So its officials decided to gentrify the neighborhood, in essence enlarging their ivory tower. Thousands of lower-income residents have been displaced as more students move into the neighborhood and rental and housing prices have doubled in the past three years. Falcon observes that he doesn't want the University to do things "for" the community anymore (2004). He wants them to help the community recognize its own goals. He also points out the dearth of spaces for local residents and college students to interact. He has long been an advocate for building community and recreational centers open to all. While the university is developing corridors of businesses around the school, he points out that they have so far failed to fund any of the badly needed recreational facilities for local youth. This is a particularly interesting point, as Philadelphia Mayor John Street has proposed closing more of the limited recreational facilities and public pools in the city to meet a funding crisis. Residents are now turning to local institutions like the University of Pennsylvania to provide what the city says it can no longer do. Is this an example of a private institution helping to maintain the public sphere? Or does it demonstrate how only private institutions can now perform the functions the state once did? In other words, is this the private sphere supporting a public one, or the death of the public?

The crucial element here is that residents feel that that is something at stake in their involvement. High crime is a fresh memory, so spikes in muggings or robberies bring out general concern and neighbors meet to analyze and develop strategies to deal with the problems. Similarly, there is a great deal of variation between different groups' visions for the neighborhood's future. If everyone basically agreed on what should happen, then there would be no strong reason for people to become involved. Additionally, since people feel that their input does have an impact, they are willing to spend time at meetings. Specific problems arise, but different groups have formed that often serve as opposing party factions. Disagreement and discord is a crucial part of maintaining an active community and motivating people to make their voice heard. This is a point made by the postmodern theorists of community I discussed in this book's introduction. But what is missing from their description is the other elements such as shared infrastructure and leadership that make such disagreement worth pursuing.

Gentrification and Danger to the Community. Interestingly, the success of the University of Pennsylvania's redevelopment of this neighborhood confirms my earlier argument that a consumer mentality can work in ways that are antithetical to community life. For example, as the elementary school that is "assisted" by the University of Pennsylvania becomes established, this means that housing prices in the "catchment area"—the area designated as the boundaries of the school—have accelerated. Families with young children cluster into these blocks, often making sacrifices to meet the higher mortgages so their children can attend the school. But in this case, parents can often act outraged when something goes wrong at the school. New homebuyers feel that the increased cost of buying their home means that they have already "invested" in both the neighborhood and the school, and they expect a return for their monetary investment. In this sense, they approach the neighborhood and the school not as participants, but rather as customers who bought a product and who demand satisfaction. As housing prices increase and more people make a financial investment in the school district, this attitude will become more predominant. It remains to be seen whether the other kinds of investment in neighborhood and school will be able to counteract this kind of attitude.

The same dynamic may hold with the neighborhood's relationship to the University. For example, in some instances when a crime occurs residents blame the University for a failure in its security, rather than looking at larger causes and becoming active. The danger in marketing a community, a school, or a business corridor as the University City Development District is now doing is that those who "buy" into it will see their initial relocation as the extent of their investment. Those who "buy" into the community, knowing that there are problems and obstacles to be overcome, understand that work lies ahead. There is a crucial distinction in response to a problem. If residents ask themselves how they can fix a problem or meet a crisis, community life will continue to thrive. Yet if more residents ask what the University is going to do about a problem or crisis, then the community life will begin to falter. In this sense, I believe the success of the renewal in the neighborhood may be its greatest danger. Not only will it decrease diversity over the long run, replacing many of those who now volunteer time, but it may also create an expectation that the neighborhood is fixed or ideal, and therefore worth purchasing at an elevated price. Once again, the idealization of a community comes at a heavy price.

Although different in their focuses, the studies of West Philadelphia and Celebration, Florida, complement the more theoretical discussions about community that preceded them. First, I began by asserting that imagination can be understood as existing in dynamic tension between the individual and the collective, the possible and the material. This position is demonstrated in community politics in West Philadelphia. Many individuals have chosen to live in the neighborhood, driven by their own vision of community involvement and membership. I have sat in meetings where different people assert their vision and others vigorously contest it. It is clear that there is no dominant and singular vision of what this community stands for. This disagreement, combined with the underlying commitment to the community itself, creates the pressing need to participate. It is the tension between individual and collective perceptions of the community that drives much of the involvement in planning, decision-making, and problem solving.

Many of the theorists of community I've discussed have argued for the importance of difference within communities. Many of these same thinkers might be dismayed by a racially homogeneous neighborhood due to concern that identities would be formed only in relation to those who are similar to one another. I believe that in practical terms, West Philadelphia demonstrates another way of understanding the reason why communities must embrace difference. Communities need money, volunteers, gardeners, lawyers, and organizers to succeed. In a place like Celebration where real estate costs are high, the majority of community members, through financial necessity, must be primarily dedicated to their careers. They have monetary resources, but this is only one kind of the investment that is needed to make a community function. Students have numbers, time, and energy to, for example, collect signatures, post fliers, and staff informational tables. Students and retirees may not have money to contribute to the community, but their time is an invaluable asset. The tragedy of current neighborhood spatial arrangements is that too often families are segregated from retirees, the underemployed are too often segregated from the overemployed. Hence their differentiated abilities cannot balance one another. Difference within communities not only provides for a different basis of identity construction, it is also a vital element in sustaining a functional collectivity.

Third, as both the Celebration and West Philadelphia examples suggest, communities need larger sponsors. Yet as most community rhetoric reveals, most Americans consider the state or government to be antithetical to the survival of communities. It is clear that grassroots efforts alone cannot help a community to thrive or be resurrected. These cases are unusual because a large and wealthy entity has stepped in to provide the funding necessary to make these projects successful. What does it say that now an Ivy League institution takes community involvement and public good as a primary mission? I am not arguing that the University of Pennsylvania is wrong to do so. But why isn't the government similarly invested in the public good? We need to conceptualize and encourage a more symbiotic relationship between community activism and government sponsorship. The only way that the lessons of special cases such as Celebration and West Philadelphia are going to be able to be put into place in more locales is if the state takes a larger role in community development and if community organizers look at the state as a potential partner.

Finally, I want to reiterate how dangerous the combination of consumerism and community seems to be. It would be impossible to have community stand as an island unaffected by the consumer culture that pervades American life today. Yet it is crucial to realize the tendency to substitute involvement for consumption, or to simply confuse the two altogether. Relating to a community as a consumer creates a simultaneous engagement and distance—community becomes something that is acquired, not achieved. In debates about the community schools in Celebration and West Philadelphia, a common complaint is that parents "bought into" the community in order to assure themselves of a quality education for their children. When something is not to their liking, they respond as if suffering from a case of false advertising. This understanding of their relationship with the school leads to an expectation that goods will be delivered, that the payment has already occurred. But no community can survive if its members assume that they have already paid their dues or that no further investment or involvement is necessary. The marketing of communities is thereby deeply antithetical to the success of these same communities. The solution isn't to insist that consumerist capitalism is different from community life, as this is simply a denial of reality. Instead, we must understand that marketing and selling an idealized community does not serve community life.

It is striking how frequently ideals of community oppose the practice of vibrant communities. Many of our ideas of community seem to be inaccurate, for instance in seeing communities as naturally harmonious or without hierarchy. The idea that community and capitalism are antithetical has proved to be pernicious, as commodity fetishism affects people's experience of community virtually every day, and generally not for the better. The demands of the labor market also make the commitment of time toward community life ever more difficult to make. So in many ways, the idealization of community life as something very different than it usually is can lead people to disengage from collective life just when they are most needed. It is precisely when there are problems and acrimony that community life becomes even more important. But we are unable to invest in these debates if we think that community is "really" about fulfillment or personal identity. This is not to say that community life, no matter how contentious, does not create identity or fulfillment, only that it does so in unexpected ways. Community cannot be envisioned as the perfect alternative to what we have. Our collective imaginary of what can be should not be allowed to interfere with the work needed to get there.

WORKS CITED

Agamben, Giorgio. 1993. *The Coming Community.* Trans. Michael Hardt. Minneapolis: University of Minnesota Press.
Alcoff, Linda Martín. 1988. "Cultural Feminism versus Post-Structuralism: The Identity Crisis in Feminist Theory." *Signs: A Journal of Women in Culture and Society* 13 (2): 405–36.
Alpert, Jane. 1973. "Mother Right: A New Feminist Theory." *Ms.*, August.
Amariglio, Jack, and Antonio Callari. 1993. "Marxian Value Theory and the Problem of the Subject: The Role of Commodity Fetishism." In *Fetishism as Cultural Discourse,* ed. Emily Apter and William Pietz. Ithaca: Cornell University Press.
Anderson, Benedict. 1983. *Imagined Communities.* New York: Verso Press.
Anzaldúa, Gloria. 1987. *Borderlands/La Frontera: The New Mestiza.* New Mexico: Aunt Lute Books.
Arendt, Hannah. 1958. *The Human Condition.* Chicago: University of Chicago Press.
———. 1963. *On Revolution.* New York: Penguin Books.
———. 1968. *Men in Dark Times.* New York: Harcourt, Brace & World.
Aristotle. 1969. *The Politics of Aristotle.* Ed. and trans. Ernest Barker. London: Oxford University Press.
Arnstein, Sherry. 1968. "The Ladder of Citizen Participation." *Journal of the Institute of American Planners* 35 (4): 216–24.
Barber, Benjamin. 1975. *Liberating Feminism.* New York: Seabury Press.
———. 1984. *Strong Democracy: Participatory Politics for a New Age.* Berkeley and Los Angeles: University of California Press.
———. 1988. *The Conquest of Politics: Liberal Philosophy in Democratic Times.* Princeton: Princeton University Press.
———. 1998. *A Place for Us: How to Make Society Civil and Democracy Strong.* New York: Hill and Wang.
Baudrillard, Jean. 1975. *The Mirror of Production.* Trans. Mark Poster. London: Telos Press.
———. 1983. *Simulations.* Trans. Paul Foss, Paul Patton, and Philip Beitchman. New York: Semiotext(e).
Beauvoir, Simone de. 1953. *The Second Sex.* Trans. and ed. H. M. Parshley. New York: Knopf.
Bellah, Robert N. 1985. *Habits of the Heart: Individualism and Commitment in American Life.* Berkeley and Los Angeles: University of California Press.
———. 1990. "The Invasion of the Money World." In *Rebuilding the Nest: A New Commitment to the American Family,* ed. David Blankenhorn, Steven Bayme, and Jean Bethke Elshtain, 227–36. Milwaukee: Family Service America.

Benhabib, Seyla. 1992. *Situating the Self: Gender, Community, and Postmodernism in Contemporary Ethics.* New York: Routledge.
———. 2002. *The Claims of Culture: Equality and Diversity in the Global Era.* Princeton: Princeton University Press.
———, ed. 1996. *Democracy and Difference: Contesting the Boundaries of the Political.* Princeton: Princeton University Press.
Benjamin, Jessica. 1988. *The Bonds of Love: Psychoanalysis, Feminism, and the Problem of Domination.* New York: Pantheon Books.
Benjamin, Walter. 1999. *The Arcades Project.* Trans. Howard Eiland and Kevin McLaughlin. Cambridge, Mass.: Belknap Press.
Blankenhorn, David, Steven Bayme, and Jean Bethke Elshtain, eds. 1990. *Rebuilding the Nest: A New Commitment to the American Family.* Milwaukee: Family Service America.
Blankenhorn, David, and Mary Ann Glendon, eds. 1995. *Seedbeds of Virtue: Sources of Competence, Character, and Citizenship in American Society.* Lanham, Md.: Madison Books.
Bradley, Bill. 1995. "Civil Society and the Rebirth of Our National Community." *The Responsive Community* 5 (2): 4–10.
Bronner, Stephen Eric. 1999. *Ideas in Action: Political Tradition in the Twentieth Century.* Lanham, Md.: Rowman & Littlefield.
Brown, Wendy. 1995. *States of Injury: Power and Freedom in Late Modernity.* Princeton: Princeton University Press.
Burstein, Rachel. 1995. "Disney Magnet School Repels." *Multinational Monitor* 16 (12).
Calhoun, Craig, ed. 1992. *Habermas and the Public Sphere.* Cambridge, Mass.: MIT Press.
Campbell, Colin. 1987. *The Romantic Ethic and the Spirit of Modern Consumerism.* Oxford: Basil Blackwell.
———. 2000. "The Puzzle of Modern Consumerism." In *The Consumer Society Reader,* ed. Martyn Lee. Oxford: Blackwell.
Chang, Grace. 2000. *Disposable Domestics: Immigrant Women Workers in the Global Economy.* Boston: South End Press.
Clay, Grady. 1973. *Close-Up: How to Read the American City.* New York: Praeger.
———. 1987. *Right Before Your Eyes: Penetrating the Urban Environment.* Washington, D.C.: American Planning Association.
Cohen, Jean, and Andrew Arato. 1992. *Civil Society and Political Theory.* Cambridge, Mass.: MIT Press.
Connolly, William E. 1991. *Identity/Difference: Democratic Negotiations of Political Paradox.* Ithaca: Cornell University Press.
———. 1995. *The Ethos of Pluralization.* Minneapolis: University of Minnesota Press.
Constable, Nicole. 1997. *Maid to Order in Hong Kong: Stories of Filipina Workers.* Ithaca: Cornell University Press.
Coontz, Stephanie. 1992. *The Way We Never Were.* New York: Basic Books.
Corlett, William. 1989. *Community Without Unity: A Politics of Derridian Extravagance.* Durham: Duke University Press.
Cott, Nancy F. 1987. *The Grounding of Modern Feminism.* New Haven: Yale University Press.

Cullen, Gordon. 1961. *The Concise Townscape.* New York: Van Nostrand Reinhold.
Dean, Jodi. 1996. *The Solidarity of Strangers: Feminism After Identity Politics.* Berkeley and Los Angeles: University of California Press.
Debord, Guy. 1994. *Society of the Spectacle.* Trans. Donald Nicholson-Smith. New York: Zone Books.
Delanty, Gerard. 2003. *Community.* New York: Routledge.
Dewey, John. 1946. *The Public and Its Problems.* Chicago: Gateway Books.
Dietz, Mary G. 1987. "Context Is All: Feminism and Theories of Citizenship." *Daedalus* 116 (4): 1–24.
differences. 1997. Special section on Parité in France. Vol. 9 (2): 69–142.
Economist. 1995. "It's a Small Town After All." August 26.
Ehrenberg, John. 1999. *Civil Society: A Critical History of an Idea.* New York: New York University Press.
Ehrenhalt, Alan. 1995. *The Lost City: The Forgotten Virtues of Community in America.* New York: Basic Books.
Ehrenreich, Barbara. 2001. *Nickel and Dimed: On (Not) Getting By in America.* New York: Henry Holt.
Eisenstein, Zillah. 1981. *The Radical Future of Liberal Feminism.* New York: Longman.
Elshtain, Jean Bethke. 1981. *Public Man, Private Woman: Women in Social and Political Thought.* Princeton: Princeton University Press.
———. 1982a. "Feminism, Family, and Community." *Dissent* 29 (4): 442–49.
———. 1995. *Democracy on Trial.* New York: Basic Books.
———, ed. 1982b. *The Family in Political Thought.* Amherst: University of Massachusetts Press.
Engels, Friedrich. 1978. "Socialism: Utopian and Scientific." In *The Marx-Engels Reader,* ed. Robert C. Tucker, 683–717. New York: W. W. Norton.
Enloe, Cynthia. 2000. *Maneuvers: The International Politics of Militarizing Women's Lives.* Berkeley and Los Angeles: University of California Press.
Erikson, Erik. 1958. *Young Man Luther: A Study in Psychoanalysis and History.* New York: W. W. Norton.
Etzioni, Amitai. 1990. "Liberals and Communitarians." *Partisan Review* 57 (2): 215–27.
———. 1993. *The Spirit of Community: The Reinvention of American Society.* New York: Simon and Schuster.
———. 1995. "Old Chestnuts and New Spurs." In *New Communitarian Thinking: Persons, Virtues, Institutions, and Communities,* ed. Etzioni, 16–34. Charlottesville: University of Virginia Press.
———. 1996a. *The New Golden Rule: Community and Morality in a Democratic Society.* New York: Basic Books.
———. 1996b. "A Moderate Communitarian Proposal." *Political Theory* 24 (2): 155–71.
Falcon, Larry, Rev. 2004. Personal interview, June.
Fanon, Frantz. 1967. *Black Skin, White Masks.* Trans. Charles Lam Markmann. New York: Grove Press.
Flax, Jane. 1987. "Postmodernism and Gender Relations in Feminist Theory." *Signs: A Journal of Women in Culture and Society* 12 (4): 621–43.
———. 1993. *Disputed Subjects: Essays on Psychoanalysis, Politics, and Philosophy.* New York: Routledge.

Fleming, Marie. 1993. "Women and the 'Public Use of Reason.'" *Social Theory and Practice* 19 (1): 27–50.

———. 1997. *Emancipation and Illusion: Rationality and Gender in Habermas's Theory of Modernity*. University Park: Pennsylvania State University Press.

Foglesong, Richard E. 2003. *Married to the Mouse: Walt Disney World and Orlando*. New Haven: Yale University Press.

Ford, Richard. 1995. "The Repressed Community." *Transition* 65: 96–117.

Foucault, Michel. 1984. *The Foucault Reader*, ed. Paul Rabinow. New York: Pantheon Books.

Franzt, Douglas. 1998. "Living in a Disney Town with Big Brother at Bay." *New York Times*, October 4.

Franzt, Douglas, and Catherine Collins. 1999. *Celebration, U.S.A.: Living in Disney's Brave New Town*. New York: Henry Holt.

Fraser, Nancy. 1992. "Rethinking the Public Sphere: A Contribution to the Critique of Actually Existing Democracy." In *Habermas and the Public Sphere*, ed. Craig Calhoun, 109–41. Boston: MIT Press.

———. 1997. *Justice Interruptus: Critical Reflections on the "Postsocialist" Condition*. New York: Routledge.

Frazer, Elizabeth. 1999. *The Problems of Communitarian Politics*. Oxford: Oxford University Press.

Frazer, Elizabeth, and Nicola Lacey. 1993. *The Politics of Community: A Feminist Critique of the Liberal-Communitarian Debate*. Toronto: University of Toronto Press.

Freie, John. 1998. *Counterfeit Community: The Exploitation of Our Longing for Connectedness*. New York: Rowman & Littlefield.

Fukuyama, Francis. 1995. *Trust: The Social Virtues and the Creation of Prosperity*. New York: Free Press.

Gilligan, Carol. 1982. *In A Different Voice: Psychological Theory and Women's Development*. Cambridge, Mass.: Harvard University Press.

Glendon, Mary Ann. 1987. *Abortion and Divorce in Western Law*. Cambridge, Mass.: Harvard University Press.

———. 1991. *Rights Talk: The Impoverishment of Political Discourse*. New York: Free Press.

———. 1997. "Feminism and the Family: An Indissoluble Marriage." *Commonweal* 124 (3): 11–15.

Glenn, Evelyn Nakano. 1992. "From Servitude to Service Work: Historical Continuities in the Racial Division of Paid Reproductive Labor." *Signs: A Journal of Women in Culture and Society* 18 (1): 1–43.

Gutmann, Amy. 1992. "Communitarian Critics of Liberalism." In *Communitarianism and Individualism*, ed. Shlomo Avineri and Avner de-Shalit, 120–36. Oxford: Oxford University Press.

———. 2003. *Identity in Democracy*. Princeton: Princeton University Press.

Habermas, Jürgen. [1962] 1989. *The Structural Transformation of the Public Sphere: An Inquiry into a Category of Bourgeois Society*. Trans. Thomas Burger. Cambridge, Mass.: MIT Press.

———. 1995. *The Philosophical Discourse of Modernity*. Trans. Frederick G. Lawrence. Cambridge, Mass.: MIT Press.

———. 1992. "Further Reflections on the Public Sphere." In *Habermas and the Public Shpere,* ed. Craig Calhoun, 421–61. Cambridge, Mass.: MIT Press.
Hardt, Michael, and Antonio Negri. 2000. *Empire.* Cambridge, Mass.: Harvard University Press.
Harkavy, Ira, and John Puckett. 1992. "Planning for the Future." *Planning for Higher Education* 20 (summer).
Hayden, Delores. 2003. *Building Suburbia: Green Fields and Urban Growth 1820–2000.* New York: Pantheon Books.
Hegel, G. W. F. [1821] 1967. *Hegel's Philosophy of Right.* Trans. T. M. Knox. London: Oxford University Press.
———. 1977. *The Phenomenology of Spirit.* Trans. A. V. Miller. Oxford: Clarendon Press.
Hirschmann, Nancy. 1992. *Rethinking Obligation: A Feminist Method for Political Theory.* Ithaca: Cornell University Press.
Honig, Bonnie. 1993. *Political Theory and the Displacement of Politics.* Ithaca: Cornell University Press.
———. 2001. *Democracy and the Foreigner.* Princeton: Princeton University Press.
Ignatieff, Michael. 1984. *The Needs of Strangers.* New York: Penguin Press.
Irigaray, Luce. 1985. *This Sex Which Is Not One.* Trans. Catherine Porter with Carolyn Burke. Ithaca: Cornell University Press.
———. 1993. *Sexes and Genealogies.* Trans. Gillian C. Gill. New York: Columbia University Press.
James, William. 1962. "On a Certain Blindness in Human Beings." In *Essays on Faith and Morals.* New York: Meridian Books.
Kant, Immanuel. 1983. *Perpetual Peace and Other Essays.* Trans. Ted Humphrey. Cambridge: Hackett Publishing.
Kateb, George. 2002. "On the Adequacy of the Canon." *Political Theory* 30 (4): 482–505.
Kessler-Harris, Alice. 1990. *A Woman's Wage: Historical Meanings and Social Consequences.* Louisville: University of Kentucky Press.
Kittay, Eva Feder. 1999. *Love's Labor: Essays on Women, Equality, and Dependency.* New York: Routledge.
Klein, Barbara (founder, St. Mary's Nursery School, Philadelphia). 2004. Personal interview, May.
Kohn, Margaret. 2004. *Brave New Neighborhoods.* New York: Routledge.
Kramer, Jane. 2000. "Liberty, Equality, Sorority: French Women Get a Revolution of Their Own." *New Yorker,* May 29.
Kristeva, Julia. 1980. "La Femme, ce n'est jamais ça." In *New French Feminisms,* ed. Elaine Marks and Isabelle de Courtivron, 137–50. New York: Schoken Books.
Kroloff, Reed. 1997. "Disney Builds a Town." *Architecture* 86 (8).
Kunstler, James Howard. 1996. *Home from Nowhere: Remaking Our Everyday World for the Twenty-First Century.* New York: Simon and Schuster.
Landes, Joan. 1998. "The Public and Private Sphere: A Feminist Reconsideration." In *Feminism, The Public and the Private,* ed. Joan Landes, 135–62. Oxford: Oxford University Press.
Lasch, Christopher. 1977. *Haven in a Heartless World: The Family Besieged.* New York: W. W. Norton.
Lily, Jim. 2004. Personal interview, May.

Lipset, Seymour Martin. 1996. *American Exceptionalism: A Double-Edged Sword.* New York: W. W. Norton.
Locke, John. 1988. *Two Treatises of Government.* Ed. Peter Laslett. Cambridge: Cambridge University Press.
Lorde, Audre. 1984. *Sister Outsider.* Freedom, Calif.: The Crossing Press.
Lugones, Maria. 1994. "Purity, Impurity, and Separation." *Signs: A Journal of Women in Culture and Society* 19 (2): 458–79.
Lukacs, Georg. 1988. *History and Class Consciousness.* Trans. Rodney Livingstone. Cambridge, Mass.: MIT Press.
MacKinnon, Catharine. 1989. *Toward a Feminist Theory of the State.* Cambridge, Mass.: Harvard University Press.
Marcuse, Herbert. 1964. *One-Dimensional Man: Studies in the Ideology of Advanced Industrial Society.* Boston: Beacon Press.
Marx, Karl. 1963. *The Early Writings.* Trans. and ed. T. B. Bottomore. New York: McGraw-Hill.
Marx, Karl, and Friedrich Engels. 1966. *The Civil War in France.* Peking: Foreign Language Press.
McCamant, Kathryn, and Charles Durrett. 1988. *Cohousing: A Contemporary Approach to Housing Ourselves.* Berkeley, Calif.: Habitat Press and Ten Speed Press.
Meehan, Johanna, ed. 1995. *Feminists Read Habermas: Gendering the Subject of Discourse.* New York: Routledge.
Minow, Martha. 1999. *Not Only for Myself: Identity, Politics, and the Law.* New York: The New Press.
More, Thomas. 2001. *Utopia.* Trans. Clarence Miller. New Haven: Yale University Press.
Mosley, Leonard. 1986. *Disney's World.* New York: Stein and Day.
Mouffe, Chantal. 1993. *The Return of the Political.* London: Verso.
Muschamp, Herbert. 1998. "Celebration." *New York Times,* October 4.
Mycek, Shari. 1998. "Wishing Upon Disney's Star." *Hospitals and Health Networks* 72: 1.
Nancy, Jean-Luc. 1991. *The Inoperative Community.* Ed. Peter Connor, trans. Peter Connor, Lisa Grabus, Michael Holland, and Simona Sawhney. Minneapolis: University of Minnesota Press.
Nietzsche, Friedrich. 1989. *On the Genealogy of Morals and Ecce Homo.* Trans. Walter Kaufmann and R. J. Hollingdale. New York: Vintage Books.
Okin, Susan Moller. 1979. *Women in Western Political Thought.* Princeton: Princeton University Press.
———. 1989. *Justice, Gender, and the Family.* New York: Basic Books.
Oldfield, Adrian. 1990. *Citizenship and Community: Civic Republicanism and the Modern World.* London: Routledge.
Packard, Vance. 2000. "Growthmanship." In *The Consumer Society Reader,* ed. Martyn Lee, 223–27 Oxford: Blackwell Publishers.
Pateman, Carole. 1970. *Participation and Democratic Theory.* Cambridge: Cambridge University Press.
———. 1989. *The Disorder of Women: Democracy, Feminism, and Political Theory.* Stanford: Stanford University Press.
Phelan, Shane. 1989. *Identity Politics: Lesbian Feminism and the Limits of Community.* Philadelphia: Temple University Press.

Phillips, Andrew, and Anthony Lorrayne. 1997. "The Disney Dream." *Maclean's* 110: 29.
Phillips, Anne. 1993. *Democracy and Difference.* University Park: Pennsylvania State University Press.
Piven, Frances Fox. 1990. "Ideology and the State: Women, Power, and the Welfare State." In *Women, The State, and Welfare,* ed. Linda Gordon, 250–264. Madison: University of Wisconsin Press.
Pollan, Michael. 1997. "Town-Building is No Mickey Mouse Operation." *New York Times Magazine,* December 14.
Putnam, Robert. 1993. *Making Democracy Work: Civic Tradition in Modern Italy.* Princeton: Princeton University Press.
———. 1995. "Bowling Alone: America's Declining Social Capital." *Journal of Democracy* 6 (1): 65–78.
Rae, Douglas. 2003. *City: Urbanism and Its End.* New Haven: Yale University Press.
Rawls, John. 1971. *A Theory of Justice.* Cambridge: Cambridge University Press.
Reagon, Bernice Johnson. 1983. "Coalition Politics: Turning the Century." In *Home Girls: A Black Feminist Anthology,* ed. Barbara Smith, 356–68. New York: Kitchen Table Women of Color Press.
Ross, Andrew. 1997. "The Mickey House Club." *Artforum* 35 (6).
———. 1999. *The Celebration Chronicles: Life, Liberty, and the Pursuit of Property Values in Disney's New Town.* New York: Ballantine Books.
Rothchild, John. 1995. "A Mouse in the House." *Time,* December 4, 23.
Rousseau, Jean-Jacques. 1964. "Discourse on the Origin and Foundations of Inequality." *The First and Second Discourses,* ed. Roger D. Masters, 77–181. New York: St. Martin's Press.
Ruddick, Sara. 1980. "Maternal Thinking." *Feminist Studies* 6 (2): 342–67.
Ryan, Mary P. 1979. "Femininity and Capitalism in Antebellum America." In *Capitalist Patriarchy and the Case for Socialist Feminism,* ed. Zillah Eisenstein, 151–72. New York: Monthly Review Press.
———. 1981. *Cradle of the Middle Class: The Family in Oneida County, New York, 1790–1865.* Cambridge: Cambridge University Press.
———. 1990. *Women in Public: Between Banners and Ballots, 1825–1880.* Baltimore: Johns Hopkins University Press.
———. 1992. "Gender and Public Access: Women's Politics in Nineteenth-Century America." In *Habermas and the Public Sphere,* ed. Craig Calhoun. Cambridge, Mass.: MIT Press.
———. 1997. *Civic Wars: Democracy and Public Life in the American City During the Nineteenth Century.* Berkeley and Los Angeles: University of California Press.
Rymer, Russ. 1996. "Back to the Future: Disney Reinvents the Company Town." *Harper's Magazine,* October.
Sandel, Michael. 1982. *Liberalism and the Limits of Justice.* Cambridge: Cambridge University Press.
———. 1996a. "America's Search for a New Public Philosophy." *Atlantic Monthly,* March, 57–74.
———. 1996b. *Democracy's Discontent: America in Search of a Public Philosophy.* Cambridge, Mass.: Belknap Press.

Sassen, Saskia. 1991. *Global City: New York, London, Tokyo*. Princeton: Princeton University Press.
Scarry, Elaine. 1999. "The Difficulty of Imagining Others." In *Human Rights in Political Transitions: Gettysburg to Bosnia*, ed. Carla Hesse and Robert Post, 277–309. New York: Zone Books.
Schudson, Michael. 1986. *Advertising, the Uneasy Persuasion: Its Dubious Impact on American Society*. New York: Basic Books.
Selznick, Philip. 1992. *The Moral Commonwealth: Social Theory and the Promise of Community*. Berkeley and Los Angeles: University of California Press.
———. 1995. "Personhood and Moral Obligation." In *New Communitarian Thinking: Persons, Virtues, Institutions, and Communities*, ed. Amitai Etzioni, 110–25. Charlottesville: University of Virginia Press.
Sennett, Richard. 1971. *The Uses of Disorder: Personal Identity and City Life*. New York: Vintage Books.
Skaler, Robert. 2002. *West Philadelphia: University City to 52nd Street*. Charleston: Arcadia Publishing.
Smith, Dorothy. 1999. *Writing the Social: Critique, Theory, and Investigations*. Toronto: University of Toronto Press.
Stacey, Judith. 1990. *Brave New Families: Stories of Domestic Upheaval in Late Twentieth-Century America*. New York: Basic Books.
———. 1996. *In the Name of the Family: Rethinking Family Values in the Postmodern Age*. Boston: Beacon Press.
Taylor, Charles. 1975. *Hegel*. Cambridge: Cambridge University Press.
———. 1989. *Sources of the Self: The Making of Modern Identity*. Cambridge, Mass.: Harvard University Press.
———. 1992. *The Ethics of Authenticity*. Cambridge: Harvard University Press.
Tessman, Lisa. 1995. "Beyond Communitarian Unity in the Politics of Identity." *Socialist Review* 24 (1–2): 55–83.
Tocqueville, Alexis de. [1835, 1840] 1969. *Democracy in America*. New York: Harper Perennial.
Tönnies, Ferdinand. [1887] 1957. *Community and Society* [Gemeinschaft und Gesellschaft]. Trans. Charles Loomis. New York: Harper and Row.
Trinh T. Minh-Ha. 1989. *Woman, Native, Other: Writing Postcoloniality and Feminism*. Bloomington: Indiana University Press.
———. 1991. *When the Moon Waxes Red: Representation, Gender, and Cultural Politics*. New York: Routledge.
Tronto, Joan. 1993. *Moral Boundaries: A Political Argument for an Ethic of Care*. New York: Routledge.
Varenne, Hervé. 1977. *Americans Together: Structured Diversity in a Midwestern Town*. New York: Teachers' College Press.
Walzer, Michael. 1990. "The Communitarian Critique of Liberalism." *Political Theory* 18 (1): 6–23.
———, ed. 1995. *Toward a Global Civil Society*. Providence, R.I.: Berghahn Books.
Weintraub, Jeff, and Krishan Kumar, eds. 1997. *Public and Private in Thought and Practice: Perspectives on a Grand Dichotomy*. Chicago: University of Chicago Press.

Weir, Alison. 1996. *Sacrificial Logics: Feminist Theory and the Critique of Identity.* New York: Routledge.
Wilson, Elizabeth. 1991. *Sphinx in the City: Urban Life, the Control of Disorder, and Women.* Berkeley and Los Angeles: University of California Press.
Wolin, Sheldon S. 1960. *Politics and Vision: Continuity and Innovation in Western Political Thought.* Boston: Little, Brown.
Young, Iris Marion. 1990. *Justice and the Politics of Difference.* Princeton: Princeton University Press.
———. 1994. "Gender as Seriality: Thinking about Women as a Social Collective." *Signs: A Journal of Women in Culture and Society* 19 (3): 713–38.
———. 1997. *Intersecting Voices: Dilemmas of Gender, Political Philosophy, and Policy.* Princeton: Princeton University Press.

INDEX

Agamben, Giorgio, 5, 118–19
Alcoff, Linda, 36
Alpert, Jane, 45
Amariglio, Jack, 113
Arato, Andrew, 61
Aristotle, 47
Arnstein, Sherry, 80
authenticity, 29–30
amour propre, 23
amour soi, 23
Anderson, Benedict, 13–15
Anzaldúa, Gloria, 5
Arendt, Hannah, 21, 22, 59, 77

Barber, Benjamin, 3, 34, 45, 59, 62, 75–76
Baudrillard, Jean, 118–19
Bellah, Robert, 62
Benhabib, Seyla, 4, 50, 59, 76–77
Benjamin, Jessica, 53
Benjamin, Walter, 1, 17–20, 22, 120
Blankenhorn, David, 49, 63
Bradley, Bill, 62
Brandeis, Louis D., 68
Bronner, Stephen Eric, 2
Brown, Wendy, 73–75
Burstein, Rachel, 93, 104

Calhoun, Craig, 76
Callari, Antonio, 113
Campbell, Colin, 113–17
Celebration, Florida, 7
  architecture, 90
  compared with West Philadelphia, 121–23
  design, 88–92
  downtown, 90–91
  political structure, 102–10
  public school, 93, 104–5
  real estate prices, 92–95
Chang, Grace, 55
civic communitarianism, 3, 45, 49, 62
civil society
  and economics, 64–65
  and public/private divide, 62–65
  different conceptions of, 61–62
  feminist critiques of, 63–64
Cohen, Jean, 61
Collins, Catherine, 87
commodity fetishism, 7, 114
  and community, 116–20
community sentencing, 2, 3
community
  agonistic vision of, 38
  debate, 134–36
  disadvantages of marketing, 137–39
  education, 123–24
  gentrification, 136–37
  involvement, 133–37
  leadership, 130–31
  multiple membership, 31–32, 35–36
  normative use, 9
  structural interdependence, 131
concrete other, 50
Connolly, William, 5, 7
Constable, Nicole, 55
consumer behavior, 112–14
Coontz, Stephanie, 51
Corlett, William, 5
Cott, Nancy, 51
counterfeit community, 113

Dean, Jodi, 63
DeBord, Guy, 116–20
Delanty, Gerard, 3

democratic despotism, 18, 106
democratic participation, 47, 71–72, 75–83
Dewey, John, 81–83
Dietz, Mary, 78–79
Disney, Walt, 93, 102–3
Disney Corporation
    as developer, 102–10
    imagineers, 89–90

Ehrenberg, John, 65
Ehrenhalt, Alan, 108
Ehrenreich, Barbara, 55
Eisenstein, Zillah, 51, 59
Elshtain, Jean Bethke, 45, 59, 62
Engels, Friedrich, 16, 60
enlarged mentality, 77, 80
Enloe, Cynthia, 54
EPCOT, 93, 104
ethics of care, 45, 50–51
Etzioni, Amatai, 4, 34, 35

Falcon, Rev. Larry, 135
family, 44
    and democracy, 48–50
    and nostalgia, 56–57
    as model for justice, 50–51
    as natural institution, 52
    as political institution, 48
    as training for citizenship, 52–57
    between public/private divide, 48–52
    in capitalism, 54–57
    in popular imagination, 56–57
Flax, Jane, 5
Fleming, Marie, 76
Foglesong, Richard, 87, 103
Ford, Richard, 25
Foucault, Michel, 24
fragmentary identity, 34–35, 36, 39
Franzt, Douglas, 87
Fraser, Nancy, 63, 76
Frazer, Elizabeth, 5
Freie, John, 113
French feminism, 11
Fukuyama, Francis, 61

generalized other, 50
gentrification, 136–37
Gilligan, Carol, 45
Glendon, Mary Ann, 4, 49, 67–69
Glenn, Evelyn Nakano, 46, 51
globalization, 4
Graves, Michael, 90
Gutmann, Amy, 25

Habermas, Jürgen, 60, 61, 64, 76–77
Hardt, Michael, 71
Harkavy, Ira, 126, 129
Hayden, Delores, 124
Hegel, G. W. F.
    end of history, 44
    master slave dialectic, 26–28, 30, 40
    ideal of the state, 66
    self-consciousness, 23, 39
Hirschmann, Nancy, 51
Homogeneity, 31–32, 33, 37, 39
Honig, Bonnie, 5
human emancipation, 66

identity politics, 30–36, 73–74
Ignatieff, Michael, 56
imagination
    and consumption, 114–15
    and theory, 85
    collective versus individual, 17–20
    hyperactive, 16
    identity, 40–41
    inactive, 16–17
    institutions, 43
    unmoored, 20–22
imaginative hedonism, 114–16
interior migration, 21
Irigaray, Luce, 36–37, 43

James, William, 39–40
Johnson, Philip, 90

Kant, Immanuel, 48
Kateb, George, 16–20
Kessler-Harris, Alice, 55
Kittay, Eva Feder, 45, 51
Klein, Barbara, 131

Kohn, Margaret, 109
Kramer, Jane, 60
Kristeva Julia, 20
Kroloff, Reed, 96, 107, 108
Kumar, Kristen, 48

Lacey, Nicola, 5
Landes, Joan, 63
liberalism
  and citizenship, 78
  individualism, 14–15
  view of state, 59
Lipset, S. M., 61
Locke, John, 12, 47
logic of purity, 31, 33, 35, 36
Lorde, Audre, 4, 25, 32, 33
Lugones, Maria, 5, 31, 33, 35, 36, 39
Lukacs, Georg, 117

MacKinnon, Catherine, 46
Marcuse, Herbert, 2
Marx, Karl, 66, 111
master-slave dialectic, 26–28, 30, 37, 38, 40
Meehan, Johanna, 76
Minow, Martha, 45, 51
More, Sir Thomas, 10, 12
Mosley, Leonard, 93, 103
Mouffe, Chantal, 59, 75–76
multiple subjectivities, 37
Muschamp, Herbert, 89
Mycek, Shari, 105

Nancy, Jean-Luc, 5, 10
nationalism, 69–71
Negri, Antonio, 71
new communitarinaism, 25
new urbanism, 87, 92
Nguyen v. INS, 54
Nietzsche, Friedrich, 21
nostalgia, 10, 11, 111

Okin, Susan, 52
Oldfield, Adrian, 75, 79

Packard, Vance, 113
Paris Commune, 60

Parité, 59–60
particularism, 5, 28, 44
Pateman, Carole, 51, 59
paternalism, 48
Pelli, Cesar, 90
phantasmagoria, 18–19, 21–22
Phelan, Shane, 24
Phillips, Anne, 5, 59
Piven, Frances Fox, 73
political emancipation, 66
Pollan, Michael, 93, 108
public/private spheres, 44–45
  civil society and, 61–63
  feminist readings of, 51
  history of, 46–47
public participation, 3–4, 75–83
public sphere, 60, 63–64, 76–77
Puckett, John, 126, 129
purified community, 97–100
Putnam, Robert, 61

Rae, Douglas, 131
Reagon, Bernice Johnson, 4, 24, 33, 34, 98
Rawls, John, 50
Reedy Creek Improvement District, 103–4
republican motherhood, 49, 51
rights talk, 67–68
Rodin, Judith, 126
Ross, Andrew, 87, 89, 95
Rothchild, John, 89
Rousseau, Jean-Jacques, 12, 23
Ruddick, Sara, 45
Ryan, Mary, 51, 54–55, 63–64
Rymer, Russ, 87, 107

Sandel, Michael, 3, 25, 50, 69–71
Sassen, Saskia, 132
Scarry, Elaine, 43
Seaside, Florida, 86, 87
Schudson, Michael, 113
Scott-Brown, Denise, 90
security, 96–100
Selznick, Phillip, 4, 29, 35–36
Sennett, Richard, 96–100
Skaler, Robert, 125

Smith, Dorothy, 85
social contract theory, 48, 52
spectacle, 116–20
Stacey, Judith, 46
state
   and participation, 81–83
   communitarian critiques of, 67–72
   feminist critiques of, 72–75
   Hegelian conception of, 66
   Marx's critique of, 66
Stern, Robert, 90, 106–7
streetcar suburbs, 124

Taylor, Charles, 29–33, 36
Tessman, Lisa, 24, 38–39
Tocqueville, Alexis de, 3, 48–49, 52, 61, 106, 109
Tönnies, Ferdinand, 3, 11, 12–15, 86–87, 111
Trinh, T. Minh-Ha, 5, 37–38
Tronto, Joan, 45, 51
Truman Show, The, 85–86

Universalism, 44, 72–73

University of Pennsylvania, 121
   mortgage assistance, 127–28
   public elementary school, 128–29
University City Development District, 127, 135–36
utopia, 10

Varenne, Hervé, 9
Venturi, Robert, 90

Walzer, Michael, 15, 23
Warren, Samuel, 68
Weintraub, Jeffrey, 48
Weir, Alison, 24
West Philadelphia, 7
   compared with Celebration, 121–23
   crime, 123
   history, 124–27
   income diversity, 123–24
   property values, 129
Wilson, Elizabeth, 51
Wolin, Sheldon, 12

Young, Iris Marion, 5, 97, 98